The Genesis of How to Pray for Your Church

Bringing Disunity into Unity

D. Rebecca Brotherton

Compiled & Edited by Mark Brotherton

Copyright © 2021, Mark Brotherton
All rights reserved.

No part of this publication may be reproduced or transmitted in any form or by any means, electronic or mechanical, including photocopying and recording, or by any information storage and retrieval system, except in the case of brief quotations for use in articles and reviews, without written permission from the copyright owner.

The views expressed in the book are the author's and do not necessarily reflect those of the publisher.

Germancreative has designed the book cover.

7710-T Cherry Park Dr, Ste 224
Houston, TX 77095
www.WorldwidePublishingGroup.com
(713) 766-4271

Cover design: http://HarvestCreek.net

ISBN: 978-1-64830-405-7

Dedication

I dedicate this book to the person who never saw her brainchild come to fruition – Della Rebecca Brotherton. I think, however, Rebecca would like to dedicate it to the Prayer Warrior. She would want it to be a reference in the library of anyone interceding on behalf of their church.

Table of Contents

Acknowledgments 1

Preface.. 2

Introduction to Genesis 4

Life Event Number 1 - Adam and Eve 11
   Prelude... 11
   Guideline #1: Begin with God 14
      A Snare in Plain Sight 15
      The Triad of Drift... 18
      Root Cause and Ramifications................................. 31
   Guideline #1 – Second Wind 39
      Church Pulling to the Left?....................................... 40
      Get an Alignment... 43
      Guideline Wrap Up: Indicator Parameters............. 46
      Guideline #1 Reprise: Begin with God, Not with Man 51
   Summary List of Prayer Pointers from Adam & Eve 53

Life Event Number 2 – Noah 57
   Guideline #2: Begin with a Sense of Purpose 58
      Through a Glass Dimly... 59
      But then Face to Face... 84

    Guideline Wrap Up: What is Your Purpose? 101
  Guideline #3: Begin with The Proper Foundation 106
    Parable of the Faithful Apprentice and the Unfaithful
    Apprentice 106
    Materials are Material: Countering Inexorable Decline 109
    What is Reality? 110
    Guideline Wrap Up: Foundational Indicators 113
  Guideline #4: Begin with Something New 115
    Can New Be Negotiated? 115
    Micromanaging vs. Macromanaging 117
    No Final Conflict 119
    Course Correction 120
    Guideline Wrap Up: Gathering our Threads on Paradigm
    Shifts 122
  Summary List of Prayer Pointers from Noah 126

Life Event Number 3 – Abraham **129**

  Guideline #5: Begin with Obedience - Do Not Despise Small
  Beginnings 130
    Broad Brush Strokes 132
    Not All of Us Can Be Charter Members 138
    Is the Sacred Really Sacred 142
    Everything is Optional 148
    Story Time 154
    Guideline Wrap Up: Casting the Past into the Future 156

Guideline #6 – Begin with Obedience – Do Not Stifle Your Faith 157
    Abram's Destiny 159
    Abram's Progeny 162
    According to Who's Reckoning? 164
    Believe the Impossible 173
    Impossible to Believe? 177
    Guideline Wrap Up: Faith & Obedience or Obedience & Faith? 180
Guideline #7: Begin with Proper Planning: Timing is Everything. 182
    Our Counsel Not Required 182
    Triage Prayer Ministries 184
Guideline #8 – Begin in Covenant with God 185
    Let's Covenant Together 185
    What is Sacrifice? Really! 188
    You Know, the Other Element? 189
    Guideline Wrap Up: Tying It Up with a Bow 196
    Summary List of Prayer Pointers from Abraham 199

Life Event Number 4 – Jacob 203

    Guideline #9: Begin with A Prayer of Release from Our Past 203
    Family Systems 204
    A Peek Behind the Curtain 205
    Fear or New Sight? 206
    Meanwhile, Back at Laban's Ranch 207

Guideline #10: Begin with A Prayer of Dedication.................209
   Between the Bookends...210
   What is Devotion? 214
   Counting the Costs 216
Guideline #11: Begin with a Prayer for Sanctification...........218
   Reciprocity?..219
   Or Quid Pro Quo?...219
   Eventually, the Buses Stop Running 221
Summary List of Prayer Pointers from Jacob 223

Life Event Number 5 – JOSEPH 225

Guideline #12: Begin with Vision 225
   Cool for Joseph..226
   Bridging the Gap...227
Guideline #13: Begin in the Face of Adversity......................229
   Why the Road is Less Traveled 229
   There Are No Storms in Spiritual Clouds 232
   My Dilemma..235
   Storm? What Storm?...237
Guideline #14: Begin with Tenacity & Perseverance.............238
   Seeing Beyond His Troubles 239
   Are Obstacles Just Distractions?................................239
Guideline #15: Begin with Integrity 240
   Let's Take Stock..241
   Cause or Effect?..242

Noah De Ja Vu 244
Guideline #16: Begin with a Pinch of Humility..................... 246
Life's Not Fair, but is it Just? 247
The Ball's in Your Court Now.. 248
Summary List of Prayer Pointers from Joseph 251

A Prayer from the Book of Genesis **255**

Genesis Summary **259**

Acknowledgments

I would like to acknowledge and thank two people who made significant sacrifices of their time to review the manuscript and provide valuable comments and suggestions. Both brought a unique relationship to the table. Paula Stratton worked with Rebecca in the "Next Steps" ministry at our church. I felt it appropriate to entrust the book's review to someone Rebecca trusted. My former supervisor at work, Paul Wild, is an author in his own right, having written on end-times prophecy, among other topics. Finally, I want to thank my God, who kept me focused on the end goal and strengthened me daily to press on toward the mark. My God is able: Daniel 3:7, Luke 3:8, Acts 20:32, Romans 11:23, Romans 14:4, II Cor. 9:8, Hebrew 7:25.

Preface

It was a seemingly routine day on the way to recovery for Rebecca. She was in the rehab center recovering from the ravages of chemotherapy. The therapy was working; the tumor was about one-half to three-quarters its original size after two treatments. But Rebecca had a weak constitution. I was visiting with her after work, and she was diligently working on the initial draft. Believing it would be a book, she made an odd comment that caught my attention, but I quickly dismissed it as a bout of discouragement. I encouraged her to work all the more diligently, thinking that would dispel the discouragement. The comment was, "... someone else may have to finish my book".

Taking note of that comment, I parked it in the back of my mind. It couldn't have been more than a few days later that they rushed Rebecca to the hospital for being nonresponsive. They were able to bring her back into consciousness for a period, but that was short-lived. From the time she arrived at the hospital, the doctors spoke of no hope and even dropped comments about making final arrangements. On the other hand, I was sure it was just a hiccup, and she would be back at the rehab facility in a matter of days. She never recovered. So, as you may have surmised by now, this book is being published posthumously.

With time, I don't know how much time, I realized I was the one that was going to have to finish her book. At that point, I picked up the torch. When I noted above that she believed it would be a book, I didn't speak of whether it would ever be published. I was speaking of how many volumes it would be. She thought it was going to be one book. When I began to compile her materials, I then realized the magnitude of effort it would entail. It was more like one volume for Genesis, one for Exodus, one for Leviticus, Numbers, and Deuteronomy combined, and so on. I don't think she had any idea of the volume of written material she had generated. But I counted the costs and deemed it worthwhile.

Through the process of wordsmithing and connecting trains of thought, much of myself found its way into the book. One of my reviewers who knew Rebecca personally picked up pretty quickly that not all was Rebecca. A quick word count before and after I got hold of it found that roughly half is Rebecca. Following is how it played out. Rebecca laid out the floor plan, poured the foundation, built the framework, and provided many furnishings. I came in and did the brickwork, put up the sheetrock, finished the interior, and brought in additional furnishings.

Looking back, this has been an odyssey for which I would trade nothing. Odysseys are life's defining experiences. Yes, there were times I felt I was striving toward an elusive goal that remained on the horizon. But that horizon in the distant future eventually crept into the present. It is now my prayer that the contents of this book will assist you and your church in whatever odyssey on which you have chosen to embark.

Mark Brotherton

Introduction to Genesis

Genesis: the book of beginnings. Its very presence in the Bible teaches us that beginnings are fundamental in the eyes of God. That is true for the Church in general and personal ministries as well. Genesis paints such a stark picture of why we should begin every day of our lives with God. It also emphasizes why everything we do should start with prayer. I believe our need to rely on prayer is more by consequence than by design. The failures and conflicts of the myriad participants in Genesis emphasize why we should begin everything with prayer. Cases in point: Eve and the serpent, Cain and Able, everyone but Noah, Ham and Noah, Nimrod and the tower of Babel, Sarai and Hagar, Abram and Pharaoh, Abraham and Abimelech, Lot and Sodom, Isaac and Abimelech (Abimelech lived a long time), Jacob and Esau, Jacob and Isaac, Jacob and Laban, Joseph and his brothers. It probably would have been easier just to name Enoch, the one success story that did not involve God's intervention. I suppose one could argue that if there were a subplot to the Genesis story, it was to let Man stand on his own to prove that he can't. As such, God's biblical narrative of His people's origins and beginnings will serve nicely as a model for our conceptions.

The biblical narrative laid out in Genesis demonstrates how the end product of God's chosen people grew out of the interplay between *consequential free will* and God's *directives and intervention*. I emphasize free will because it appears God gave the Genesis players a lot of latitude in making their own choices and setting their courses. Most of these ended poorly. By contrast, their successes were due solely to God's intervention on their behalf. Consider Jacob; God doesn't intervene when Jacob scams Esau out of his birthright and blessing. But after fleeing Esau and arriving at Uncle Laban's house of shifting sand, God most assuredly bails him out when things get hopelessly fouled up there. I encourage you to read Jacob's full story to see firsthand how Jacob's life played out in this regard.

I relegate parts of Genesis to the category, "You made your bed now lie in it." Case in point, Jacob has to leave home after cheating his brother Esau out of his birthright and his blessing. We learn of this in Genesis 27:42:

Surely your brother Esau comforts himself concerning you by intending to kill you.

I relegate other parts of Genesis to the category, "I need you for My purposes, so I'm intervening in the wreck your life has become." Continuing with Jacob as our example, Uncle Laban pursues Jacob for "stealing" his herds. We read of this in Genesis 31:24:

But God had come to Laban the Syrian in a dream by night and said to him, "Be careful that you speak to Jacob neither good nor bad.."

In bringing this concept contemporary with our day and time, the viewpoint I've woven into these pages is that we are incapable of not making a wreck out of our lives.

Concerning prayer, Genesis invites us to look at the issue of beginnings in a very genetic fashion. That is because our genetics force us to make do with what we bring into this world. That's a complicated way of saying we can't escape the heritage handed down to us through the generations from Genesis to the present. Of course, I'm speaking primarily in terms of spiritual genetics. However, biological genetics plays an essential role, as will be pointed out when considering Jacob's contribution to our subject matter. In this regard, my mind harkens back to my favorite statement by Zig Ziggler when commenting on those of us with conflictual personalities. "No matter where you go, there you are." The same principle applies to our churches, which are genetically inept, simply because **we** make up the Church. Addressing the gravity of this inherited condition quite naturally calls for frankness. So, when confronted with the choice of being diplomatic or candid, I lean toward the latter. I choose frankness to communicate an unmistakable message: The Church is not the author, originator, supplier, or finisher of righteousness. Stated differently, being born again does not make us independently righteous. To break the monotony of gravity, however, I will interject humor from time to time.

The principles and concepts we garner from Genesis teach us a couple of things:

1. The strength and character of our church is a function of our interaction with God, and

2. God does not automatically disqualify us from service when we make poor decisions but can put us back on track to continue our pilgrimage.

In the latter, one could argue whether God will preserve His name by intervening against the congregation's will. I think not because of the number of churches that exist, but that's about all they do. But if God does intervene, it probably won't turn out well for the leaders that set a course contrary to God's will. The same goes for those churches where the leadership is on track, but certain factions oppose the leader in some respect. It will not go well for those who oppose God's anointed. I've seen it with my own eyes.

We will look at prayer elements through the life stories of Bible characters, which I have termed Life Events. Our roster of Life Events for Genesis will feature the following characters along with the associated elements or attributes they best exemplify:

- **Adam and Eve:** Begin with God
- **Noah:** Begin with a Sense of Purpose
  Begin with the Proper Foundation
  Begin with Something New
- **Abraham:** Begin with Obedience – Do Not Despise Small Beginnings
  Begin with Obedience – Do not Stifle Your Faith
  Begin with Proper Planning: Timing is Everything
  Begin in Covenant with God
- **Jacob:** Begin with a Prayer of Release From our Past
  Begin with a Prayer of Dedication
  Begin with a Prayer for Sanctification
- **Joseph:** Begin with Vision

> Begin in the Face of Adversity
> Begin with Tenacity & Perseverance
> Begin with Integrity
> Begin with a Pinch of Humility

For each life event, I will touch on:

1. <u>Scriptural Theme:</u> scriptural support for the guideline.

2. <u>Target Populations:</u> Who is impacted the most by the issue under review.

3. <u>Topical Delineation and Elaboration:</u> The real-world context constraining us.

4. <u>Membership Focus:</u> Tips specifically intended to target you or your congregation.

5. <u>Key Insights for Prayers:</u> Discussion themes distilled into prayer pointers.

For brevity, the term "Prayer Pointers" is used interchangeably with "Key Insights for Prayer." The latter are used as headings to list these insights. Prayer Pointers are the informal equivalent used in the text. Regarding scriptural support, I quote from the New King James Version (NKJV) unless note otherwise. Also, I don't limit scriptural support to Genesis. To comprehensively understand the concepts presented, I also bring New Testament scripture into an Old Testament discussion.

Concerning Target Populations, these are not to exclude all other groups in your church; they are just the principal targets. The dynamics of church operations prevent a restrictive definition of a Target Population.

One might construe the premise of "beginnings" as limiting the target audience to those establishing a new church from scratch. The principles, however, can also apply to any church starting a new ministry initiative. Possible initiatives might include a new mission church across town or a new ministry in their existing facilities. Growing church bodies are always open to something new. So beginnings are limited only by the *life* and *vitality* of your church. You will notice that I did not say *imagination*. The attribute of imagination doesn't dictate God's direction; God dictates God's direction. Your sensitivity and response to God's calling complete the deal. That is why life and vitality are the two critical attributes your church needs to have. So, if your church is low on these qualities, you will benefit from this book.

As we proceed through the various facets of prayer, I will use two approaches to give you a greater depth of understanding of how to pray for your church. In the first, I may appear to chase rabbits or go off on tangents that have little to do with prayer. I am doing neither. Instead, I am vicariously imparting experiences I've endured to expose many of the pitfalls that beset ministries. These are pitfalls I've seen, heard, and experienced in the church over my lifetime. In the second, I place you in the position of decision-maker on the direction your church takes or how it conducts business. I'm not presenting a "how-to" manual. Decision-making is not just an objective process. It's also an emotional process that carries with it the burden of consequences.

I want to pause a moment and comment on God's direction and calling. Over the years, I've occasionally heard how people couch God's calling in terms of man's recognition of an opportunity, as though the idea originated with man. Phrases like, "it would have never happened if Pastor So-and-So had not recognized the need and stepped up in meeting the challenge." As a prayer warrior, you need to start getting used to the fact that it is the other way around. God is sovereign, and He isn't bumping around in the dark like we are.

Following the last Life Event, I reassemble Prayer Pointers into a summary list representing all Life Events. The book of Genesis will then be closed out with a poem for your edification.

I know God Has Great Things for you! It only remains for you to see them so you can claim them and know what to pray for in experiencing a great beginning.

So fellow prayer warrior, let's begin our journey of discovery.

Life Event Number 1 - Adam and Eve

Prelude

Applicability

- **Target Population:** Church Body at Large

Topical Delineation and Elaboration

Adam and Eve's world was so perfect. Today, our world will never even approach such a standard of perfection, nor can we even imagine how splendid that must have been. Adam and Eve were most familiar with the delightful blessing of communing directly with God – the benefit of unhindered access. Have you ever considered how that was the norm for them and not the exception? No doubt, their Lord came to have fellowship with them regularly. They knew they were God's people and very near and dear to his heart.

And then the Fall.

Consider the contrast. Amid paradise, Adam and Eve committed an act in absolute discordance with what that paradise represented. And not even the aesthetic perfection of the Garden of Eden could cloak Adam and Eve from discovery, for it was in the cool of the day when the Lord confronted them in their transgression. Try and envision the juxtaposition of these two conflicting paradigms.

In the aftermath, Adam and Eve likely did not fully understand the concept of prayer as we know it today. By contrast, I'm sure they would view our understanding of pray as wholly obscure. Of a certainty, the loss of unhindered access probably sent them reeling, placing them at a total loss of how to compensate for it. They were entering uncharted territory insofar as communing with their creator. Despite this limitation, however, the Lord seems to leave the door cracked open. They seem to retain the privilege of communicating directly with Him, but not as free and unhindered as before. Nevertheless, after the Fall, it's likely that their understanding of prayer quickly became more aligned with our comprehension of prayer than it was with their experience before the Fall. For this reason, Adam and Eve are an excellent study since they saw life from both sides of the Fall.

Membership Focus: *We, too, are God's people, and we are very special to him. Do we have any legitimate justification for thinking that we are any less remarkable to Him than Adam and Eve were? Yet, we use the fact that sin separates us from God as justification that we are less exceptional.*

In repudiating this mindset, the Cross is irrefutable proof that God desires to have fellowship and communion with us as well. I hardly think the Cross would have ever occurred if our premise were so. Whereas the Lord clothed Adam and Eve in the skins of animals sacrificed for their sake, He clothes us in the righteousness of His Son whom He sacrificed for our sake. He would not have made this sacrifice if our separation made us less special.

As a result of that sacrifice, He accomplishes fellowship with us through prayer. He has established prayer as fully as it will ever be in this life. God no longer restricts access through a Jewish priest in the line of Aaron. On what basis can we so confidently assert this? On the basis that Christ removed the middle wall of partition that limited fellowship during the extended period between the fall of man and the Cross of Christ. That is a physical reality expressed in Luke 23:45b: *the veil of the Temple was torn in two*. Thus, the scope of possibilities is much broader now. The potential is far greater, and the number of people who can tap into this resource is phenomenal.

Where, of all places, can this tremendous potential be realized? The obvious answer is the Church at large. Because of the Cross, the Church by definition comprises God's people. Hence, this tremendous potential is realized only by the Church – God's people assembled in vast numbers. As a side note, when speaking of the local body of Christ, the term "church "will be used interchangeably with "congregation, "membership," and "church body."

Membership Focus: *As God's people, adopted through the vehicle of salvation, we are His representatives, and for that reason alone, we should strive for excellence. That is our responsibility. Indeed, we can't undo the Fall, so we can't fellowship with God as Adam and Eve did. As the Church, however, we should nevertheless pursue our goals with this mentality and spiritual ambition. Therefore, the church will be our context of choice for expanding on the principles of prayer. There we will explore the topic and* *what God's word continues to say to us. We shall also contemporize some ancient principles that we can apply to the church as well.*

In this discussion on the global context of prayer, the target population is logically the church congregation, not just the leadership. That is because of 1ˢᵗ Peter 2:9: *But you are a chosen generation, a royal priesthood, a holy nation.* Let's stop here and have our first prayer pointer.

Key Insight for Prayer: Pray that the congregation will realize that prayer is their responsibility and domain. It is not the purview of only "the anointed," the leadership, or the Prayer Team. It is not just the domain of those we tout as skilled in the Art of Praying.

That brings us to our first guideline.

Guideline #1: Begin with God

Applicability

- **Target Populations:** Church Staff and Lay Leaders

Topical Delineation and Elaboration

This guideline is appropriate because, *In the beginning, God - Genesis 1:1*

When we begin with God, we will have a taste of paradise, just as Adam and Eve did. God will always bless us to some degree. In pursuit of this goal, the church that desires to follow His will should not undertake any endeavor or ministry unless God sanctions it. We should take no steps forward until we have prayed them through, asked our heavenly Father how to execute them and what he wants us to do next. Just because it's God's will does not mean He has already blazed the path forward or that it is guaranteed success or without peril. Hence, we ought always to begin everything with God. The premise of Guideline #1 is not just for those planting a church. Congregations that have been around a long time can also benefit from this guideline. It applies to any new initiative or ministry you have in the idea or planning stages.

A Snare in Plain Sight

The Set-Up - Begin with God. At first glance, you may think this is an odd directive to make when addressing God's people and especially the Church. However, there is a logical explanation behind it and what we need to pray for concerning our churches. The heart of the matter lies in what we rely on the most in the initial stages of our church's attempt to begin its ministry. In reality, *most* churches begin with the very best of intentions. They certainly wouldn't attempt to establish a new work unless it originated with God. They seek God's direction through prayer, and everyone believes in God for the best. That church takes God's marching orders and runs with God in accomplishing them.

They know they are embarking on uncharted territory and are excited to take the risk because they believe God is in their court. For this reason, *most* churches have extraordinary beginnings, so you might think this guideline is somewhat patronizing. There is one situation in which this scenario may not hold, new churches springing up due to church splits. These churches might not start up because God showed them a need; they might originate from disagreements with the church leadership. I would classify some of these churches as having improper beginnings that are less than stellar. But, that doesn't mean they can't be a legitimate church. After all, Paul and Barnabus had a disagreement, which resulted in a ministry split. Irrespective of how a church starts, there is another problem. Beginning with the very best of intentions doesn't work.

The Lure - Just what is the nature of this problem? How does it enter the picture in the first place, and how do we deal with it? It's very subtle and can easily blindside us because we don't know how to look for it. That's why our prayers are so critical in dealing with this particular something.

Recall the statement above that Adam and Eve saw life from both sides of the Fall. They began with God, but something got in the way. What was that something? Churches always launch with God when they start a new work, but often, something gets in the way. Again, what is that something?

In Adam and Eve's case, that something was the *lure of being like God.*

What about in our churches? Is there any parallel to Adam and Eve's case? Absolutely! In our case, that something is *precisely the same thing* - the *lure of being like God.*

It just expresses itself differently. We don't recognize it as the lure of being like God, but it is. That is why beginning with the best of intentions doesn't work. In pitting the "best of intentions" against the "lure of being like God," there is no contest, the latter will always win, and it has time on its side.

The Trap Springs - We don't recognize it as a problem because it is so insidiously familiar. It's not apparent because it's like a comfortable shirt; you feel at home in it, which is why it is so insidious. We can call it the *Comfort Factor*. Don't take the Comfort Factor lightly; it's a prominent blind spot that hampers our spiritual growth if we aren't aware of it. And that is why it causes immense difficulties within the church body. How can we as Christians learn to recognize it, how can we define it, and how can we pray about its prevalence in the church? Let me walk you through it.

Most Christians who have been around a long time would probably agree with the following picture I'm about to paint. Over time churches drift away from God, despite the best intentions, and they don't just drift for no reason. Remember when I stated above that *"the heart of the matter lies in what we rely on the most?"* In the process of drifting, reliance on God becomes displaced by dependence on something else. In the case of our church bodies, a subtle shift from a trust in God to dependency on man takes hold of the congregation. Let me restate it in a different light. Over time, there is a subtle shift from reliance on **God, Whom we can't see**, to dependence on **man, whom we can see**. Most of what you need to know lies in the bold text.

This manifestation is multifaceted and complicated, but it can be traced back to one root cause for all its complexities. Before we get into the root cause, I want to touch on three major component areas where we permit drift to manifest itself. I term these:

1. Celebrity Leadership Focus
2. The Business Model Framework
3. The Expert Bypass

All three of these are interrelated and can segue from one to the other. Let's cover each component individually and address the dynamic interrelationship under the umbrella of strongholds.

Life Event Number 1 - Adam and Eve

The Triad of Drift

Celebrity Leadership Focus - Man and human personalities begin to displace God and overshadow the Lord in this component. Ministries and programs shift their focus from God to a gifted pastor or minister with a charismatic personality. Hence, the term celebrity leadership focus. The pastor does not necessarily do this by design; it just happens. That is, it's not premeditated. I will elaborate on the phenomenon of how "it just happens" later.

In other instances, this condition can focus on an elder, deacon, Sunday school teacher, or other influential church members who dominate the church's leadership landscape. In still other cases, the central personality may not have any personality. It's Mr. Deep Pockets, the one who provides substantial funding to the church – and of course, he has his opinion on how to conduct church business. This latter scenario is more appropriate in a related discussion below. However, I want to include it here in the list of factors that can cause a church to shift its focus. After all, we are just human, and it's easy to be captivated by a human personage. Keep descriptors such as charismatic, dynamic, gifted, and leader in the back of your mind. They all play a significant role in the dynamics of any church body, and it's probably not the role of which you are thinking.

With time these charismatic individuals progressively superimpose their will over the Father's will. Simultaneously, God's presence and leading systematically take a back seat. Again, this happens despite our good intentions. How does this happen? On the surface, it is partly the heady experience of success and the glory it brings. This exhilarating sensation persistently tugs at our leaders (and us) to take the credit (i.e., the lure of being like God). The result is a split focus between God and their success. The first step in drifting away from God is <u>a divided focus</u>.

An important clue that a church is being captivated by Celebrity Leadership is when we hear more frequent mention of man's name rather than God's. An unintended side effect is that the church membership becomes overly dependent on Reverend Personality. They come to believe he will always have their back and that his congregation is his life. For the present, that may be true. Everything is perpetually present tense insofar as the future of church leadership. Unfortunately, the pastor has not mentored an understudy or protégée who can serve as a successor. That results in inadequate preparations for future leadership of the church. So, the church flounders when Reverend Personality leaves.

Of course, there are the deacons and elders. But they generally serve only as caretakers until they find a new pastor. Consequently, the church body behaves as though they are rudderless. This practice of not selecting an understudy is the opposite of examples set in scripture: Moses and Joshua, Joshua and Caleb, Elijah and Elisha, David and Solomon, and other prominent Bible characters. Park this element of dependency in the back of your mind. I want to return to it later.

The good news is that even though a church may not have had an optimal beginning or may have drifted off course, they do not have to end that way. God can transform a church's attitude and heart. He can convert their entire way of thinking, feeling, and believing, and their way of acting. This transformation takes place only by renewing our minds through Christ and His Word (Romans 12:2). I don't give this counsel lightly or flippantly, so please don't dismiss it as just spouting biblical rhetoric. As espoused in Romans 12:2, our transformation requires us to spend time before the

Father's throne, earnestly beseeching him to instill this Christian mindset in us. May our work for Him also be characterized in this manner. Let us pray this into existence. So, the critical point to this discussion is that getting your eyes on Man can have dire consequences for your church body. Regretfully, it can eventually result in its demise.

Now let's extrapolate to the extreme. What happens when we have a renegade pastor or leader? While this can bear directly on how to pray for your church, it is tangential to the direction I want to take our discussion. So, I point you to Matthew 18:15-17, which provides broad guidelines for handling such a situation. However, to address the reason for raising the subject, I ask the philosophical question: Will God allow a pastor to become renegade? If there is a presumption within the church body that it's unnecessary to pray for the pastor because God has his back, does God have his back? I think we have a mistaken impression that those higher up the leadership ladder don't need prayer because their anointing shields them from failure. That's not true.

Contrary to our "better judgment," God does use men and women to achieve his objectives. The downside is that it's easy to get drawn into a charismatic leader's high and lofty schemes. Beginning with Man or with God will always determine the quality of spiritual life in your church. Commencing with any degree of human dependency will only dilute the spiritual quality of any endeavor you undertake for Christ and result in the church losing its saltiness.

A couple of side notes before we move on. You may recall that the Target Population for this guideline is church staff and lay leaders. You may also have noted that my discussion implicates the church body as much as the pastor. The reason for this inclusion is integral to the concept of what a leader is. We don't admit pastors into our congregation with the idea of leading them, although Lord knows we try. We receive them with the idea of following their lead, whether we agree wholeheartedly with that lead. For this reason, *as the leader goes, so goes the church body.*

The Business Model Framework - In the previous section, we talked about how the glory of success causes pastors to split their focus between God and their success. That is the first step in drifting away from God. In this state of divided attention, they proceed to the second step. They become increasingly distracted with *the maintenance required to sustain their success.* That, in turn, causes them to spend less time in an active attitude of partnering with God. In this sense, they become overly invested in their success, to the point that time spent maintaining their success displaces time with God.

As they progress further down this road, they increasingly approach the endpoint of making only logistical decisions that are "entirely reasonable" or "practical" to man. Most of these decisions have to do with available funds. It sounds odd to cast the term "entirely reasonable" in a negative light. But that is part of our problem; we operate on what we believe to be entirely reasonable in the physical realm. We let the physical constraints of the world we live in call the shots. We make few or no faith-based decisions. I will bring balance to pragmatics below, but for now, I want to concentrate on the destructive side of pragmatics.

A church's growth declines when it travels down the road of displacing attention toward God with attention to details. We eventually reach the point at which growth barely keeps pace with attrition, thereby remaining somewhat static in membership. At this stage in their pilgrimage, churches shift from the spiritual to the

Life Event Number 1 - Adam and Eve

material, which expresses itself in the pursuit of needed upgrades to keep the facilities current. The leadership holds tight to their money and is less willing to step out in faith for ministries that may be out of their financial reach. It doesn't take much of a logical leap to realize that this scenario results in a relentless decay cycle for the church body. In the end, the church is too busy fighting for survival to worry about ministry opportunities.

Don't confuse this attention to money with James' declaration that the love of money is the root of all evil. In the context in which I'm speaking, it's not the love of money; it's the dependency on money. That can apply to any church irrespective of wealth. I like to characterize it by saying expensive toys require expensive maintenance. Hence, affluent churches can have the same financial headaches as non-affluent churches in a cycle of decay. They become saddled with choosing what is more important, paying the bills, or supporting ministry initiatives. These are the churches where logistics and pragmatics reign.

Typically, being blessed financially by God is not wrong. The emphasis and reliance upon material things are what can cause us to err in the faith. I understand and support the idea that the general public will be more likely to attend your church if the facilities are well-appointed and updated. Unfortunately, for the pragmatically driven church, that is probably their only drawing card. If you had to choose one, which would you rather hear: "I think the church is spiritually strong, but their facilities are old and in need of renovation." Or "They have elegant facilities, but the general mood is oppressive and feels like death on the half shell." There is no reason you can't have the best of both worlds. But the spiritual component should be the dominant priority, and well-appointed facilities should be subordinate. Otherwise, your facilities come to own you in the form of keeping up with the times.

Again, retain the idea of dependency in the back of your mind. As a personal example, there was a period in our life when we stopped tithing because we were having financial difficulties. Our reasoning was, "God will understand." He understood alright. He understood that, at a minimum, we didn't trust him to provide, and at best, we thought that He bought off on our belief that He was no more capable of providing for us than we were. The entire scenario I've painted up to this point is what my forebearers have traditionally termed "walking by sight and not by faith," which leads to our next prayer pointer.

Key Insight for Prayer: Pray that every church within your sphere of influence always builds upon Christ and his Word. Similarly, pray that every ministry, from its inception onward, always builds upon Christ and his Word.

Membership Focus: So, does your church run its ministry more like a business rather than a God-given institution fully trusting in Him and His Word? Is your decision to launch a ministry usually determined by finances, not God's leading? I call this a knee-jerk reaction in which the flesh reacts to the price tag and tries to overrule the Spirit. Don't underestimate these knee-jerk reactions as being harmless childish behavior; they can cause church splits. I will testify of one in a Life Event later on in Genesis. Pray that this will never be the norm for your church. If it is the case with your church, pray that your fellowship will repent of this ungodly belief and practice. As with celebrity leadership focus, the root of the problem is the same - the flesh. A church built on things of the Spirit is always in sharp contrast to the church built on things of the flesh. As a Christian, and especially as a prayer warrior, your spirit will

Life Event Number 1 - Adam and Eve

bear witness with God's Spirit that you are on track. We will talk more about building on foundations under Noah.

I probably could have short-circuited much of the discussion above if I had stopped at the words "logistical decisions" in the first paragraph under *The Business Model Framework*. That pretty much sums it up because the term "logistical" implies that which is logical or practical to man. So, business decisions boil down to practically available funds, i.e., predictable funds based on the congregation's giving habits. Thus, the leaders decide to hire someone or purchase new assets based on predictable sums of money, not whether these assets are needed to fulfill a ministry vision. In the business meetings of a church where I was once a member, I can still hear Mrs. Parks chastising us in her Scottish accent, "Where is our faith?" That always brought the meetings to an abrupt halt until the awkwardness became too much to bear, then they would resume arguing where they left off.

As promised, here is the flip side of pragmatics. In situations where you are tempted to subordinate faith to logistics for weighty decisions, neither do you want to ignore logistics because it sounds spiritual. Are your decisions justifiably logical or justifiably spiritual? How do you balance the two because there is a logistical role in spiritual matters? Like it or not, when Adam and Eve were cast out of the garden, they and their descendants (meaning us) were thrown into an economic existence that depends on logistical constraints and restraints. We have to labor to earn money to buy food and shelter. We have to raise money to build our churches and keep them maintained. We have to raise more money to hire our pastors and staff. There is no free ride - ever.

On the one hand, I've been preaching about walking by faith in opposition to logistics. But on the other hand, you need to have a firm conviction to overrule logistics in favor of faith. That is, you have to be pretty confident that the ministry you don't have the money for is of God. How do we reconcile the two? Here is how. As alluded to earlier, the spiritual component needs to be the *Master*. The logistical component needs to be the *slave*.

The Expert Bypass - As a church becomes more invested financially, there is more at risk. The church now has more to lose if something goes wrong. This ties into the discussion above, where the leadership and perhaps the congregation begin to take ownership of their success, resulting in their investment owning them. When our assets come to possess us, the leadership becomes more image-conscious. They become concerned with who is populating central positions in the various ministries.

At the inception of any church, anyone can obtain approval to do anything. All that is required is that you are 98.6° and willing. As the church achieves that most important milestone of having its own facilities and becoming highly visible in the community, public perception and liability concerns start taking hold. Rank and file laity become systematically displaced either by "degreed, paid professionals" or high profile laity. Once that becomes the driver, it automatically establishes the criteria expected of the laity in presenting that image to the general public. There is a lot of financial risk at stake now. The danger here is if you do not have the personality the leadership looks for, it doesn't matter what spiritual gifts God Almighty has given you. The decision-makers will overrule, ignore or put you off, despite your willingness and desire to serve. Being put off is their favorite because that avoids the messy situation of immediately dashing someone's hopes and dreams.

Instead, the church leadership (including lay leaders) goes outside their congregation to procure professionals for the paid positions. Most reading this right now are looking at me askance and asking how else you will do it? Stay with me; let me first lay the groundwork for my explanation. Over time, the church develops a fixation with bringing in highly decorated "qualified experts" to give their ministries a quantum boost. Typically these experts are hired to create state-of-the-art programs around specific focus groups (children, youth, singles, etc.). Again, without being consciously aware of it, they progressively depend on man's expertise as the source, supplier, and provider of their needs.

It's an easy trap to fall into because people think they rely on God indirectly by trusting in someone God has endowed with the skills to do the task. But riddle me this, how many times have you seen a "Best Qualified Candidate *Called of God*" arrive at your church with great fanfare just to be gone within a year or two? What happened there? I have seen it, and I have seen it many times. Do you think God gifts people in our congregations so they can sit down and shut up in deference to an "expert" called by a search committee and is gone in a year? In one of the many venues in which visiting pastors came to my church, one gave a succinct definition of precisely what an expert is. An expert is anyone with a briefcase that is fifty miles from home. That definition follows in the same vein as the grass being greener on the other side of the fence. In other words, experts are no more special than skilled or talented people in our congregation!

So here is my answer regarding paid professionals and gifted laity. I'm not objecting to having paid professionals fill crucial positions, and I'm not wholeheartedly objecting to going outside the church in some instances to hire a qualified individual. I object to the practice that our entire pool of candidates comprises people with briefcases fifty miles from home. There appear to be few laypeople within our larger congregations being raised into those positions. No, I don't advocate sticking an inexperienced person in a principal place (paid or unpaid). However, I do endorse a mentor/mentee program for each position, similar to what they did in Old Testament times, e.g., Moses & Joshua, Elijah & Elisha, etc. And every mentor should groom their respective mentee with the intent of having them take the ministry reins if the occasion should require. Of course, the decision to pay these individuals would be at the discretion of the church leadership and the individual themselves.

Let me push a little harder on this idea. What percentage of the church population comprises seminary graduates? Now, what percentage of the church population includes lay Christians who have no spiritual gifts? That was a trick question. So, I ask again, do you think God gifts people in our congregation so that they can sit down and shut up in deference to an expert? I'm pushing hard on this because I think we have a genuine problem with professional clergy being "called of God," and they are gone in a year or two. Either God called them, or He didn't. So, who messed up? That was not a rhetorical question. Who messed up? Please do not email me your answer.

Do I think churches should *not* seek out the best of the best? Yea, pretty much. I don't know; am I just naïve, or do I need to enter the 22nd century and come to grips with the fact that spiritual gifts are archaic and have gone the way of horse-drawn carriage? That was extreme sarcasm. Calling on skilled and knowledgeable individuals in specific service areas is not inherently wrong. We err in that we disproportionately depend on these experts rather than

God, who gave these individuals their talent and know-how. It also deprives most of the laity of exercising their spiritual gifts because they are not "technically qualified."

Let me close the loop on one of the many things I told you to park in the back of your mind. In the second paragraph under *Celebrity Leadership*, I said to *"keep descriptors such as charismatic, dynamic, gifted, and leader in the back of your mind. They all play a significant role in the dynamics of any church body, and it's probably not the role of which you are thinking."* I was referring to the belief that God instilled these attributes to equip church leaders to lead. As such, don't regard these attributes as enemies of the faith. They are like tonsils; they are supposed to benefit us. Sometimes, however, they can go over to the other side and hurt us by leading us to depend on the person bearing the gift and not the God who gifted the person.

Membership Focus: *By application, the seminary did not instill these characteristics. Laypeople in your church have these same attributes and can step up into vital positions with a bit of encouragement. However, most won't rise to the challenge because we are conditioned to think leaders need to have a seminary degree or some claim to authority not held by most. However, I would add that many laypeople I've seen step into leadership positions decided to go to seminary to become better equipped. The moral of the story is that leaders should make seminary; seminaries should not make leaders.*

Now. I shouldn't promote any hair-brained idea without success stories to back it up. My church will serve that purpose. In the words of Jesus, we speak of that which we know. Do you know how we got our current Sr Pastor? We raised him from within our ranks. He started as the music minister, and we promoted him from that position to Campus Pastor. After our Sr. Pastor answered his call to missions, we elevated the Campus Pastor to Sr. Pastor with a standing ovation. Do you know how we got our current financial officer? We promoted him from church elder. Do you know how we got our Teaching Pastor (who fills the pulpit on alternate Sundays)? We elevated him from Youth Pastor. Do you know how we got our current campus pastors? We raised them both from within, one from the laity and the other from the youth leadership team.

So, you see, I know. I'm not throwing out a high-sounding idea without supporting evidence. You can ding me on the point that probably no one within our church walls mentored any of these individuals. Most were initially brought in by search committees and came into our church to fill paid staff positions. But they weren't gone within a year or two or three. And their promotions have left vacancies that, in turn, have been filled by laypeople from within. Of course, I'm sure their predecessors mentored them in one way, shape, or form to fill those positions. Ok, I'm through bragging.

Closing Arguments for Strongholds - In the discussion above, there is a subtle progression of moving God from leader to counselor, or in the vernacular, moving Him from the driver's seat to the backseat. As presented, the process advances toward making decisions based increasingly on man's ideas and philosophies (jargon for man's limitations). And speaking of philosophy, here is a philosophical question. How do drivers regard directives from back seat drivers? I won't patronize you with the obvious answer. Throughout this progression from God-led to man-led, the leadership sincerely thinks and believes they are doing what is best for the church. They erroneously believe they remain close to God and are horrified at anyone who would assert the contrary.

This entire process occurs through a phenomenon called creep (verb form). Another popular term for this process is incrementalism. In this latter state, you could say their mindset is to receive God's marching orders and run with them in their own strength because that's what they think they are supposed to do. A compelling argument given by people of this mindset is, "that is what God gave us brains for." I want to offer an alternative viewpoint on that argument. God did give us brains to operate in context with spiritual matters and, yes, social issues. However, He intended our brains to function within the framework of sinless creation like Adam and Eve before the Fall, not as devious, scheming supplanters after the Fall. Anything that gets filtered through our common sense becomes distorted by our sinful nature and comes out corrupt. The first lesson God ever taught me was why our righteousness is as filthy rags. It's because our motives are as filthy rags. Most importantly, our common sense is a function of our limitations with implicit disbelief in God's lack of constraints.

So, I would be careful about falling back on the statement, "that's what God gave us brains for." A suitable substitute would be, "that's what God gave us the Holy Spirit for," at which point everyone will turn and look at you like you are crazy. Matthew 12:34 says, *out of the abundance of the heart the mouth speaks.* So, people (whether laity or leader) will always unwittingly expose their true beliefs if you are willing to have ears to hear and listen to their speech. A dead giveaway is when anyone in leadership uses the phraseology, "I don't think we should take the church in that direction." Can you tell me what is wrong with this phrasing? If a junior employee of any business said, "I don't think we should take the company in this direction," how would be their peers respond? "I agree, but that's not our decision to make."

Now here is the tricky part. While we should not proceed without instructions from above, putting no trust in common sense, there is a caveat: Knowledge gained from our experience. That is, experiences God leads us through. The ability to take this knowledge, apply it, and put it into practice in a virtuous manner is the definition of wisdom. Here is the benefit. Once God shows us how to do something right the first time, He doesn't need to repeat the lesson. He is not in the business of micromanaging us throughout our lives. Still, neither does He want us to run ahead of Him into unknown territory.

Membership Focus: *If you are in your first church planting experience, all I preached before is valid. But if you are in your second or third church planting experience, the know-how gained in your first experience should apply in subsequent plantings. You shouldn't have to wait on God to show you how to perform repetitive tasks from one church plant to the next. You may have to wait on God to tell you when to launch, but not how to launch.*

So, while I've gone way beyond the beginning stages of a church plant, every prayer warrior needs to know the trajectory a church will probably take. Otherwise, there is no understanding of the dynamics that govern drift. Now let's get into the "why" of all this.

Root Cause and Ramifications

It's in Our Nature - In church jargon, a shift from reliance on God to dependence on Man is called operating in the sin nature or operating in the energy of the flesh. You may have heard the same concept expressed by the term "carnal." The phrase I will use to describe this phenomenon is *flesh-driven*.

I'm jumping ahead to Exodus, but think of when the children of Israel arrived at the Promised Land and sent in their scouts. Was their follow-up decision to not enter Canaan a logistical decision or a spiritual decision? The flesh-driven decision was to turn away. That was a "completely reasonable" decision. However, do you remember what happened after Israel declined to go into Canaan and God told them to head back to the desert? With the specter of returning to the dunes before them, that's when they decided to make the spiritual decision to enter Canaan. But God was not with them in that decision, and they got beaten back by the locals.

Membership Focus: *Are the decisions your church makes defensible? Whether those decisions are logistical or spiritual, can they be justified <u>spiritually</u>? How can you know the answer if you're part of a flesh-driven church?*

A flesh-driven church is just that, a pragmatically driven church. God is not allowed access except to the extent that *He submits* to the church leadership's agenda. Please don't think I'm so naïve as to believe this is an intentional stance by the church leadership; it's not. It comes in the guise of an "entirely reasonable" decision. The Pastor or leadership then declared it as ordained of God. This unconscious projectionism finds its strength in the fact that a flesh-driven church will never agree with and align itself with God's plan. The keyword here is projectionism. We project our agenda onto God as though it was God's idea revealed to us. I cannot overemphasize the fact that the flesh will never, ever back down or submit to counsel that rebuffs, rebukes, or otherwise discredits its intent.

Life Event Number 1 - Adam and Eve

Membership Focus: *When you oppose flesh-driven decisions, you might think you are confronting godly men and women. You may believe they are merely naïve about the consequences of their opinions or choices. And you may be right. But please don't allow the "godly" or "naïve" character traits to disarm you. While the "godly" quality is admirable, and we may excuse the "naïve" attribute, don't let these character traits lull you into a false sense of security. It's the fleshly component that keeps a low profile until we expose its intentions. Then it will rear its ugly head and rebuke you like you cannot imagine and without compassion or diplomacy.*

People, irrespective of their spiritual maturity, have memories. Any confrontation on your part could have future consequences, such as keeping you out of any leadership positions – like the prayer coordinator position. As a prayer warrior, you may be absolutely sure God has called you to lead the prayer ministry in your church. But, if you've had run-ins with church leadership, it may not happen, or at a minimum, your effectiveness is limited.

This brief storyline brings out my point that your ministry, by its very nature, will put a target on your back by the enemy. And the enemy uses well-meaning people in your church to do his bidding. Hence your best approach may be to maintain low visibility. That doesn't mean you should seek to be invisible or keep your viewpoints secret. It does mean that you shouldn't act as the "town crier" against flesh-driven decisions. In this regard, ask yourself whether being a vocal opponent is a <u>necessary</u> component of your job description as a prayer warrior. Let God, not you, run interference against their fleshly agendas to the extent your convictions allow.

The Dynamic Spectrum - The scenario presented thus far paints a picture that illustrates two endpoints of a spectrum into which all churches fall. One endpoint is the phenomenon of fully operating in the Spirit, i.e., starting with God and continuing with God. At this endpoint, we say they are "walking by faith and not by sight." The opposite endpoint is the phenomenon of fully operating in the energy of the flesh, i.e., relying entirely on man. We typically express the latter by going through the motions of church services, Sunday school, and routine weekly activities and ministries. Our spirit is not in it, and there is no realization of Ichabod (translated: the glory has departed from Israel). We term this latter endpoint as "walking by sight and not by faith."

Don't assume that where a church is now is where it has always been. The point where you observe them is a snapshot in time on their journey toward one extreme or the other. It is critically important that you understand no church is static. Depending on the leadership's leanings, there will always be a dynamic shift in one direction or the other.

While I introduce the concept of beginning with God under Adam and Eve, the ramifications of what it means (i.e., Spirit vs. flesh) will serve as the entire book's underpinnings.

In discussing where a church stands between these two extremes, I want to stress how churches are fundamentally motivated by the spirit or the flesh. These are the two root causes or forces for how churches progress in their development. Understanding these two drivers will help you apprehend how to pray more effectively. You will be able to recognize their fleshly or spiritual tendencies in an instant. Near the end of this Life Event, I summarize each camp's respective characteristics. These will help you recognize when a church ministry performs more with a godly emphasis or a human emphasis.

Our Teaming Arrangement - To understand the precise import of the statement, "operating in the sin nature" or "operating in the energy of the flesh," couch it in context with 1st Corinthians 9:23. That passage tells us that *no flesh shall glory in His presence*, revealing the impossibility, as well as the absurdity of trying to operate a church in the energy of the flesh. The real dilemma should thoroughly sink in when we realize that our sinful nature is *never* wholly eradicated until we reach heaven and see Jesus (I Cor. 13:8-12 & II Cor. 3:18).

So, one might counter that all is pointless. No! All is not pointless! In that regard, we can lessen our discouragement by adopting an appreciation of the following two truths.

1. We should never forsake a clear awareness that only God has the "words of life" and
2. God works within our imperfections and limitations.

Now I am well aware of scripture that says we have the mind of Christ (1st Corinthians 2:16) and that we have a new nature (2nd Corinthians 5:17). But these are in context with a spiritual walk, not a carnal walk. With this backdrop, dare we decline to team with God on the basis that we can't do anything of our own accord while we continue to reside in sinful flesh? To borrow from Francis Schaeffer, "How shall we then live?" (1976). How shall we then live spiritually despite these undesirable tendencies? More importantly, how should we pray in light of the seemingly impossible situation of this discordant relationship? Let's pause here to draw out some prayer pointers from our discussion thus far.

Key Insights for Prayer:

1. Pray for people to be challenged from the pulpit and every corner of your church to live holy lives. As the Church, we have undeniably drifted away from this concept, perhaps for any number of reasons, but chiefly because we believe it's not necessary since we live under grace.

2. Pray for a spirit of humility and contrition that prompts church members to repent early on when they realize they have sinned and need to make reconciliation, whether with God or man. In accounting parlance, we need to keep short accounts with God and all we come in contact with regularly. We should be eager to prayerfully ask for cleansing and His forgiveness instead of avoiding it because we feel unworthy or unaccountable.

3. Ask God to let us never forget what He saved us out of and from where we came. This third one is very tricky. It walks a fine line between thriving under a spirit of contrition and humility and subsisting under a perpetual burden of condemnation and guilt. That is why I place it before prayer pointer # 4, and I would also couch it in terms of the fourth prayer pointer.

4. We need to continually ask God to help us see ourselves as God sees us. That is possibly the most difficult to comprehend.

I consider these foundational prayer pointers because, without these, you might as well forget the rest. They deal with getting right with God first and then with Man. Now, I recognize I may be hitting a hornet's nest with the following comment. But, I've noticed over time that church culture has gradually transitioned into a Romans 6:1 mentality, ignoring the last clause of this passage. I respond to that comment with James 1:17b: *the Father of lights, with whom is no variation or shadow of turning*. By interpretation, God's moral code doesn't change with societal norms.

Some Basic Theology: Our Position - Concerning the fourth prayer pointer, how does God see us exactly? I've heard this statement all my life. From the conversational context, there is a presumption that God sees us as filthy, worthless sinners. The unspoken implication is when we see ourselves in a similar light, our hearts will break, we will cry and repent, and everyone goes home happy. If that's the case, then that is tantamount to denying the work of Christ. A byproduct of the whole reason He came is to deliver us from that sense of condemnation and worthlessness.

A visiting pastor once described it as dropping your burden at the Cross as you stop for a rest and then picking it back up as you continue on your journey. No dears, God does not see us that way. Not really. To see ourselves as God sees us, we must understand our position in Christ. Ephesians 2:6: *And God raised us up with Christ and <u>seated us with him</u> in the heavenly realms in Christ Jesus (NIV)*. Do you see yourself sitting in the heavenly realms?

Despite how we see ourselves, God sees us through the filter of Christ Jesus. As Christians, God sees us as perfect through the redemptive filter of Jesus Christ. If you consider it critically, that is the only way it could be. That is the *only possible outcome* of a *faultless God* executing a *faultless solution* of sacrificing His *faultless son* to pay the penalty for *hopelessly faulty humanity*. This dynamic sets up the perfect balance between two positions. One of living under the umbrella of grace (knowing our sins are paid in full) and the other embracing our responsibility under Romans 6:1:

What shall we say then? Shall we continue in sin that grace may abound? <u>*Certainly not!*</u> So, to see ourselves as God sees us is to set our face toward righteous living (the Romans 6:1 part). In this endeavor, we strive not to fall into condemnation and guilt when sin sneaks up and waylays us from the rear (the guiltless part).

With this framework, "how we should then live" is laid out in Philippians 3 and punctuated in 3:16: *to the degree that we have already attained, let us walk by the same rule.* Understanding this dynamic encompasses the four core prayer pointers listed above.

Now, if you want to get into the subject of how Jesus and the Holy Spirit see us, those may be different matters. If I were Jesus, I'm sure I would know it every time a sin check hit my bank account. And I have no idea how the Holy Spirit could not know when we sin when He has taken up residence in us. As Paul admonishes us, *do not grieve the Holy Spirit* (Eph. 4:30). Unconfessed sin grieves the Holy Spirit, thereby hindering His ability to use us. He did not save us so we can be *free to sin* with impunity. He did not redeem us to *sin that grace may abound.* He did save us for *good works* (Eph. 2:10). For that reason, we should be eager to ask prayerfully for cleansing and His forgiveness. The whole point of this discussion is that we *realize* we have been delivered from condemnation, guilt, and impossible expectations so that we are free to become more like Christ.

Thus far, woven into the discussion are a few secondary concepts that I've captured in the following prayer pointers. These are corollary prayer pointers to the four core prayer pointers.

<u>Corollary Key Insights for Prayer:</u>

1. Pray that your church will make God its beginning point in all it does.

2. Pray that Man's philosophy of pragmatism will not seduce your church.
3. Pray that your church body will discern when they rely on the flesh and understand the futility of relying on fleshly strength.
4. Pray that the church body will understand the dynamic principle of living in the flesh under grace while striving to walk in the Spirit.

Membership Focus: *When you pursue these four conditions, wrapped up in who you are in Christ, you will significantly increase your possibilities of living a life that's pleasing to God.*

Bottom line: your church needs to know what it means to trust more in an infinite God and less in Man who is finite. That is to say, be aware of what it means to walk in the Spirit and not in the flesh. Or, as we noted above, understand what it means to walk by faith and not by sight. We are to place our trust and confidence in God and God alone. For no other foundation can anyone lay than that which is laid, which is Jesus Christ (1st Corinthians 3:11). As an intercessor, you should pray that such things become a living reality in your church's membership.

Guideline #1 – Second Wind

Bear with me a little longer; we still have a few more foundational stones to lay before concluding our discussion on Adam and Eve. At this juncture, let's revisit Guideline #1 and revise it to complete the thought:

Guideline #1 Revised: Begin with God, <u>Not</u> with Man.

Church Pulling to the Left?

Priorities - In the context of our discussion to this point, beginning with God encourages us to establish our focus carefully and to recognize our priorities. I want to emphasize the word "recognize" here because, in the context in which we are speaking, we do not *establish* our priorities; we *recognize* them.

The directive to "begin with God" is our priority. All the downstream details regarding finances, logistics, coordination, personnel, etc., fall into place under this one priority. These downstream details are not our responsibility to establish or fulfill, just to carry out. It's human nature to think it's our responsibility to develop the ways and means to accomplish the visions God gives us. That frustrates us, causing us to shift our priorities from <u>trusting</u> God to <u>managing</u> our resources. Or should I say blindly managing our resources? That's because we don't know whether we should step out on faith for a grander vision or scale down the one we have according to the resources we have in hand. That potentially relegates the ministry to the category of undernourished at best and Luke 14:28 at worst.

When I say, "begin with God," we generally don't say we won't begin with God; we just don't voice it. Instead, we make our church resources the priority, and in so doing, we start with Man.

As we leave the topic of priorities, here are two prayer pointers that touch on our struggle between trusting in finances and trusting in God.

Key Insights for Prayer:

1. Pray that your church leadership can balance the role of finances in all their faith-based decisions on church operations as a whole. The importance of that is new ministry opportunities are not the only demand in your church's budget.

2. Pray that your church leadership will recognize that finances and other resources are God's vehicles to achieve His vision. Pray that they will spend more time seeking His guidance rather than the finances to carry out His plan.

More Basic Theology: Roman Chains - Now, with what is probably the most crucial point in this entire discussion, let's bring our conversation to a convergence point on this concept of the flesh vs. the Spirit. If you are in the church planting stages of development, these principles are obviously for you. For established churches, determining where you stand in the spectrum described above can be difficult. Overcoming the fleshly momentum built up over time can be even more difficult. While painful, and in some people's eyes, an unacceptable sacrifice, churches in this condition may have to go back to their roots to discover where they went wrong.

Here is an appropriate place in our discussion to give you an incredibly insightful scripture passage. I have found it to provide an acute understanding of the dynamic relationship between the flesh and the Spirit. You will be able to telescope throughout history from the beginning of man to the present and clearly understand why various individuals made their choices. You will understand why ancient Israel could never get it right. And, for that matter, us too. Oh, it's better than Romans 3:23(*all have sinned and fall short of the glory of God*). Romans 3:23 is past tense and says what we've done, but it says nothing about why we have sinned or whether we will sin again. As a spoiler alert, I've already explained in detail the principles of the passage I'm about to reveal, so it should all crystallize into a clear picture when you read it.

The passage I'm talking about is Romans 8:7:

For the sinful nature is always hostile to God. It never did obey God's laws, and <u>it never will</u> (New Living Translation).

In a nutshell, we can never train our fleshly nature to submit to God's will. Nor can we compel it to ever cooperate in carrying out any church ministry, no matter how neutral or innocuous it may appear. Our fleshly nature will render the ministry in a way that is neutral or nonthreatening to the secular system. The process of neutralization is inevitable, inexorable, and relentless. When I made the statement earlier, "God uses men and women," I prefaced it with the remark, "contrary to our better judgment." I did that for a reason. Have you ever been to Wednesday Night Prayer Meeting in a flesh-driven church? They eat dinner, have a devotional or protracted business meeting, and the prayer time gets relegated to a closing benediction. Whereas Romans 3:23 tells us what we have done, Romans 8:7 tells us why we have done it and why we will continue to do it and why we, in and of ourselves, can't do anything about it.

Membership Focus: *You and your prayer warriors need to have a clear grasp of Romans 8:7 to understand why fleshly creep or fleshly incrementalism is inevitable in any church. If unchecked, it will result in a powerless, lukewarm church that is salvageable only through a dramatic spiritual awakening and spiritual renewal.*

You and your team of prayer warriors need to have a clear grasp of Romans 8:7 to understand the mental and spiritual fog of fleshly control. The church leadership may not be able to recognize the need for spiritual awakening and spiritual renewal. The recognition may rest on you and you alone if you aren't in the same dilemma as the leadership.

And finally, you and your team of prayer warriors need to have a clear grasp of Romans 8:7 when approaching your leadership. If you bring the need for spiritual renewal to your leadership's attention, they likely will not embrace your idea. Nor will they heap accolades upon you for your incredible spiritual insight and astuteness. It will be something that will start in the prayer closets of you and your fellow prayer warriors.

Get an Alignment

Common Cause and Cure – We see two principle drains on the flesh in our preceding discussions: power and money. Some pastors face others, such as succumbing to vices like substance abuse or running off with their secretaries. But power and money are the main ones. Now, if you think the two are unrelated, they're not. They both arise out of the flesh's desire for <u>control</u>. The flesh desires control partly as a means of security and partly because it just likes to be in charge. No one operating in the flesh wants God to tell them what to do or how to do it.

Discovering how to recognize the indicators and signs of health in the church body is essential. However, acquiring and maintaining this health is another thing. Prayer is by far the most valuable tool to help followers of Christ accomplished this goal. The defeatist says, "About all we can do now is pray." That is a clear sign of surrender. It indicates that the speaker puts more faith in man's ability to fix something than God's capability or willingness. They genuinely don't believe that prayer is effective. The catch is how to pray and how to pray effectively.

Membership Focus: *If you suspect that your church is not on track, what is the solution? As I've elaborated above, don't confront your leaders or go up against them in an adversarial manner. You will be going up against the Lord's anointed if you do. Not even David went up against Saul because he recognized Saul as "God's Anointed," even when he knew Saul was wrong. That approach is nothing more than flesh going up against flesh. That is equivalent to the adage: "when you fight fire with fire, all you get is a bigger fire."*

The Catch – Again, recognizing the indicators and signs of health in the church body is essential. Discerning when to step out on the vision God has given you is crucial. And understanding how to balance faith with pragmatics is necessary. That gives us three requisites. Again, the catch to addressing all three is knowing how to pray and pray effectively.

I'm talking about earnest prayer, not the conversational prayer we exercise in group settings. There**'s a place** for that.

I'm not talking about the invocation or benediction type of prayers. There's a place for that.

And I'm not talking about the type of prayer where we populate the entire session from beginning to end with one petition after another. There**'s a place** for that.

Beginning with God has an even deeper meaning than the words written above.

Life Event Number 1 - Adam and Eve

As Christians, we have become automated in prayer. Without realizing it, we go through the motions of verbalizing requests, hoping against hope that maybe, just maybe, God will take note and deliver on this one. In reality, we have little hope that He will because we genuinely don't believe.

Blessings & Curses - But as Anna spoke blessings and curses to Mary, so also, will I speak blessings and curses to you. Reiterating what I said above, I believe we can have a taste of paradise when we begin with God. We will always be blessed to some degree when we maintain our focus going forward beyond our beginnings. However, because we now live in a fallen state, that taste of paradise will be fleeting. Enemies from within and enemies from without will eventually mar the successes won through beginning with God. But not beginning with God would be an exercise in futility.

Beginning with God won't insulate us from naysayers that hinder us from starting a good work. But it will ensure that we are launched on schedule and in the right direction.

Beginning with God won't isolate us from the pressures to conform to the World. But it will guarantee a foundation whose builder and maker is God.

Beginning with God won't prevent the trials and birth pangs of starting a new work. But it will give us the momentum that propels us through those trials.

Following is our wrap-up for Guideline #1. Here and in subsequent chapters, wrap-ups condense the salient points of some of the more lengthy guidelines.

Guideline Wrap Up: Indicator Parameters

Up to this point, I have been establishing a foundational context in which you will be operating. Regarding beginnings, one needs to be keenly aware of one specific fact I have spoken at length. The enemy of the Church is the secular mindset. That mindset which resides in the World also resides in each of us who make up the Church. We *cannot* trust it, and *it will* engage in an endless pursuit to bring the Church into subjection to its fallen nature.

As promised, the following are indicator guidelines that allow us to recognize whether a church has developed a man-like focus or a godly one. I have divided them into characteristics of the flesh-driven church and the spirit-driven church. Don't look for a one-to-one correspondence between the two categories. Noticeable attributes of the flesh-driven church may not have equivalent counterparts in the spirit-driven church.

The Flesh-driven Church

1. **It's a question of conversational emphasis and frequency.** Church members will often speak of their charismatic leader(s) and give them credit for the church's successes and blessings at the expense of giving God the glory. The Bible is true: *a tree is known by its fruit (Matt. 12:33b)*. They give lip service to God, but the fruit is how they render their ministries. That points to the one in whom they trust.

2. **It's a question of reliance.** Churches develop a fixation on bringing in highly decorated "qualified experts" to get specific ministries back on track. That includes building state-of-the-art programs around specific focus groups (children, youth, singles, etc.). However, in defending this

approach, it indeed walks a fine line between depending more upon man's expertise as a source, supplier, and provider and relying on God for these same things. The difference is that flesh-driven churches rely on the vehicle God provides and not on the God that provided the vehicle - a prime example of the Master-slave Principle.

3. **It's a question of image.** The leadership and ministry personnel will be very image-conscious and appearance-seeking. There is more of a preoccupation with impressing man with outward appearances than with devotion to God. A companion characteristic is that flesh-driven churches tend to let materialism supplant godliness. They don't trust God to provide, so they think they have to maintain well-appointed facilities to draw in paying parishioners.

4. **It's a question of what is palatable.** God's Holy Word is diluted in such a way that it is palatable to men. Otherwise, that would make them accountable, and they may have to give up some bad habits. The pure, unadulterated word of God is not what they can bear to hear. Because of Romans 8:7, they will be receptive more to man's ideas than God's ideals.

5. **It's a question of pragmatics.** Logistical decisions are based more on the secular business model or mindset than a faith-based approach.

6. **It's a question of what drives us.** Flesh-driven churches have lost their sense of purpose and the God-given vision they had at the beginning of their ministry. Here again, based on Romans 8:7, they can't maintain their sense of purpose when fleshly values and reasoning take root.

7. **It's a question of belief.** Listen to the heart of people in planning and business meetings. They speak their convictions whether they know it or not. Do they argue against ministry initiatives based on resources that are not at hand nor available, or do they promote a ministry vision on the basis that God will provide? The former shows they rely on man more than on God, and they look more to their church leadership and so-called experts to solve their problems. The latter, however, can be ambiguous. It can show legitimate faith, or it can show blind faith. Make sure God has called; otherwise, your whole justification falls apart. Yet another philosophical question, how do you distinguish which is true:

   ➢ "I don't think the Lord wants us to pursue this ministry because all of the visible indicators are wrong. There is no money, no leader, and major obstacles are blocking our path forward."

   Or

   ➢ "The Lord has planted this vision in our hearts, and we need to trust Him for the resources, the leadership, and a clear path."

   Either one could be legitimate. The answer is this: does your spirit bear witness with His Spirit. The following indicator guideline goes hand in hand with this one.

8. **It's a question of spiritual isolation.** Prayer is seldom mentioned except in passing or is assigned a subordinate or supporting role instead of a critical role. These churches certainly look good on the outside when you attend a worship service. But upon closer inspection, they tend to be

very mechanical and go through the motions. Their atmosphere is not dominated nor saturated by the Holy Spirit. It can come across as ranging from non-descript to downright oppressive. We will say more about this particular point when we delve into Exodus and the subjects of bondage and deliverance.

9. **It's a question of "real."** This guideline is synonymous with number 7 above, but in number 7, the people make no pretense; here they do. Listen for lip service to God not supported by actions. I include high-ranking members who put James to shame in the oratory prowess of their prayers. Yet, they never exhibit a faith walk either in their personal lives or at church. We tend to believe what comes out of their mouth because we can't imagine that they may be disingenuous in their spiritual walk. One key indicator I pick up on is when people refer to themselves as "mature Christians." That's usually a dead giveaway that they want to be seen as established but probably aren't. I know because I've done it myself. Every time I've told myself that I was mature, I ran across a truly mature Christian who made me look like a child playing in a sandbox. So, I quit telling myself that.

I can sum up these nine indicators in the statement "what pleases the flesh rather than what pleases the Spirit." But this carries little weight with flesh-driven churches because the flesh doesn't care.

The Spirit-driven Church

1. **It's a question of image.** The spirit-driven church is far more concerned with what God thinks than what man thinks. They are more occupied with God's heart than with outward

appearances. Having a beautiful church with ornate surroundings is to showcase God, not attract deep pockets. At the invitation of a dear friend, I once visited Lakewood Church in Houston, Texas, when John Osteen was pastor. While standing in the foyer with my host, I was taking in the ornate décor. My host noticed this and commented that John Osteen wants to present the best to honor God. The unspoken implication was that he wasn't doing it to boost membership; there is a vast difference.

2. **It's a question of emphasis.** The spirit-filled church will be conscientious to give the word of God its due prominence and elevate it to the place where it belongs in its ministry. The inerrant word of God will not be just a catchphrase. It will be the principle upon which the church solidly stands as the foundation of their ministry.

3. **It's a question of credit where credit is due.** The spirit-filled church will often have a historical review laid out by its pastor and leadership for the congregation's benefit. It will focus on how God walked with them through the years and got them where they are today.

4. **It's a question of "Sight."** The Spirit-filled church will have an established sense of purpose, and their mission as conveyed by God will be clear. Their vision will be very vivid, and it will guide them through each day.

5. **It's a question of what is not reasonable.** Spiritually minded churches will make their decisions based on faith and not on a stockbroker's risk-reward mentality. That does not mean they cast practicality to the wind and succumb to indebtedness. It does mean they will achieve a balance between these two extremes. The critical driver is a faith

certainty of what God wants versus projecting our pragmatic capabilities onto God. Yes, finances are essential, but the spirit-led church balances the two extremes by making God the Master and finances the slave.

6. **It's a question of prayer.** A Spirit-filled church will make prayer a high priority. They will understand that to do otherwise is to default to man's reasoning to carry out their mission, even if God initially established that mission. Such churches stand with an open-door policy to pray for the membership, particularly following the worship service. Spirit-driven churches I've attended typically make prayer personnel available following the worship service for anyone who has a need.

I can sum up these six attributes in the statement "what pleases the spirit rather than what pleases the flesh."

Reiterating our first guideline with scripture:

Guideline #1 Reprise: Begin with God, Not with Man

Psalm 118:9: *It is better to trust in the Lord than to put confidence in princes.*

Pray for God to teach His people the facts and reality of this proverb

Let's conclude this first Life Event with some central closing remarks and a summary list of prayer pointers.

1. Is your church flesh-driven or spirit-driven, and how do you know?

2. If you are part of a flesh-driven church, there is no shame in recognizing that. It does not necessarily mean you are flesh-driven, but it could mean you have been placed there for a reason.

3. Express your love for the church daily. Be faithful and diligent in the word. Prayer never fails.

4. Whether you begin with God or with Man will determine the quality of your ministries and their future destiny.

May God ever increase these minimal guidelines from my prayers by multiplying them many times over in your prayer life.

Summary List of Prayer Pointers from Adam & Eve

➤ **On a corporate level, pray that your church body**

- Will make God its beginning point in all it does.
- Will not be seduced by man's philosophy of pragmatism.
- Will realize that prayer is their responsibility and domain. It is not the purview of only "the anointed," the leadership, or the Prayer Team. It is not just the domain of those we tout as skilled in the Art of Praying.
- Will recognize when they rely on the flesh and understand the futility of relying on fleshly strength.
- Will understand the dynamic principle of living in the flesh under grace while striving to walk in the Spirit.

➤ **At the Leadership level, pray that your church leadership**

- Can balance the role of finances in all their faith-based decisions on church operations as a whole.
- Will recognize that finances and other resources are God's vehicles to achieve His vision.
- Will spend more time seeking His guidance rather than the finances to carry out His plan.

➤ **At the individual level, pray that each member**

- Will be challenged from the pulpit and from every corner of your church to live holy lives.

- Will keep short accounts with God and all they come in contact with regularly. They should be eager to prayerfully ask for cleansing and His forgiveness instead of avoiding it because they feel unworthy or unaccountable.
- Will be clothed in a spirit of humility and contrition that prompts them to repent early on when they realize they have sinned and need to make reconciliation, whether with God or Man.
- Will never forget what He saved them out of and from where they came.
- Will learn what it means to thrive under a spirit of contrition and humility versus subsisting under a perpetual burden of condemnation and guilt.
- Will see themselves as God truly sees them.

➢ **On a grand scale,**
- Pray that every church within your sphere of influence always builds upon Christ and his Word.
- Pray that every ministry, from its inception onward, always builds upon Christ and his Word.

Life Event Number 1 - Adam and Eve

Life Event Number 1 - Adam and Eve

Life Event Number 2 – Noah

Good old Noah! In the well-known childhood story Noah and the Ark, we find our next component of successfully praying for our church. It also fits the framework for initiating programs and ministries your church plans to institute or has already established.

Noah's Ark and its construction must have been a phenomenal task. The Scripture doesn't tell us how long it took, only that it was during the period when he was 500 to 600 years old. He surely must have been awed by the finished product, even if he did do it himself. However, one must wonder about the multitude of obstacles and setbacks between this impressive masterpiece's initiation and completion. For that reason, we do know that anyone undertaking such a monumental task would have to be unequivocally certain that God called him to do so. Most of us would agree that being told by God to do something is all the motivation Noah needed. But was that enough to make him see it through to the end? I can't tell you the number of times I was inspired to do something just to have it end up half-finished. So aside from the initial kick start, how did God incentivize Noah to see it through to the end? That brings us to our second guideline

Guideline #2: Begin with a Sense of Purpose

Applicability

- **Target Population:** The Church Body and You by Extension

Romans 8:28: *And we know that all things work together for good to those who love God, to those who are the called according to His purpose.*

Topical Delineation and Elaboration

In the Introduction, I noted that

> "*I will use two approaches to give you a greater depth of understanding of how to pray for your church. In the first, I may appear to chase rabbits or go off on tangents that have little to do with prayer.*"

Guideline #2 is what I had in mind when I made that statement. In this guideline, I use the iceberg principle to impart a comprehensive understanding of purpose, the visible and the invisible. As you are probably aware, the iceberg's visible part is only about 10% of its total mass. The vast majority of the iceberg floats below the water surface and is necessary to uphold the 10 percent above water. Applied to the concept of purpose, I attempt to characterize the invisible 90% that sustains the visible 10%. I seek to describe the more massive unseen foundational aspects necessary to support the less massive observable characteristics. With this approach, I hope to expose the inherent instabilities in the prevailing perception of ministry foundations. In so doing, I intend to bring an equally comprehensive depth of understanding to associated prayer pointers that might otherwise appear mundane or pedestrian.

Through a Glass Dimly

Purpose encompasses various levels, despite its apparent simplicity. Its dissection opens up an enigmatic awareness, best expressed best by Churchill: "It is a riddle, wrapped in a mystery, inside an enigma." (1939). So, in one respect, we can compare it to navigating a house of mirrors; in another, we are trekking through dense, wooded terrain. For simplicity, I will designate both as mazes. In his essay Self-Reliance (1841), Ralph Waldo Emerson states, "It's not the Destination, It's the journey." For us, the challenge of navigating our maze is as significant as the destination.

I won't start with a textbook definition of purpose; instead, I will begin where I believe most of us reside conceptually. I will start with a common perception of purpose that is bound up in the circumstances. In arriving at our goal, i.e., a comprehensive understanding of purpose, we will transition through various levels in a progressive order. Key mileposts along the way include:

- What We See
- What We Don't See
- What is Your Mooring Point?
- What it Means at the Corporate Level
- What it Means at the Individual Level

Of course, it wouldn't be a lesson from Noah without his perspective, so I will bring him into the discussion to clarify how the question of "why" is wrapped up in the concept of purpose.

That is, why are we doing it? At the practical level, we will discuss what should go into crafting a purpose statement. There is one scenic detour I take, and there is one rabbit I confess to chasing. So, without further ado, let's engage.

What We See - What is the concept of purpose. What does it look like for those of us starting a new ministry? Our first pass in evaluating purpose will be an aerial view, say 30,000 ft. I will use various synonyms interchangeably to provide a balanced portrayal, such as goal, meaning, and objective.

Let's begin by asking, "Where is the starting point for a ministry?" Many churches might consider the starting point as developing a formal statement that serves as the guiding principle for the new ministry. Oddly enough, if you peruse your church's founding documents, you are not likely to find a Purpose Statement per se. You are more likely to find Mission Statements or Vision Statements, or both. If you care to go to that much effort, it shouldn't be difficult to find such documents on the internet since most, if not all, churches post their statements on their website. I retrieved the Mission Statement for my church, and here is what I found:

- **Our Church Mission:** The *XYZ church* is all about making disciples who go and make other disciples.
- **Our Children's Ministry Mission:** Our Mission at *XYZ church* is to reach, teach and train kids to be Disciples.

Wow! That's a pretty heady directive – making kids into disciples.

Here is the challenge. Can you read these Mission Statements and see *purpose* or meaning embedded in either? That wasn't much of a challenge, was it? Given the simplicity of both statements, it's somewhat apparent that *making disciples* is our purpose. That's our goal and our aim. That's where we find meaning. You may notice that the Mission Statement for the Children's Ministry reads a lot like our church's Mission Statement. That's because making disciples is the overarching theme or purpose for our church, so every core ministry under our banner will be compatible with that mission directive. No matter which ministry you choose to examine at my church, it should have some variation of "making disciples" in its Mission Statement.

Here is another statement I found on our website. It's doesn't carry the title of Mission Statement, but it acts like one. It appears to be an extension of our Mission Statement.

> We are better *together* – Our promise to you is that we will be a *community* of believers who *relationally disciple* people and who *demonstrate* the love of Christ to those in our communities and around the world. We will celebrate with you, help *encourage you as you grow in Christ,* and we will *do life together.* (italics added for emphasis)

Strategic phrases like *"relationally disciple"* and *"encourage you as you grow in Christ"* add a new dimension to the idea of purpose. They add new meaning beyond mere instructional discipleship.

So now, what is our purpose? Is it to disciple, be in community or grow in Christ? Or is it hierarchal in the sense that we rank these three elements, or perhaps it has a compound goal - *to foster growth in Christ in context with community*? That was also relatively simple to figure out since it is kind of hard to instill Christ-like qualities apart from some form of community.

I also decided to step outside and look at Mission Statements from a couple of other churches. One Mission Statement and one Vision Statement are reproduced below with modifications to protect the churches' identities.

Mission Statement: We seek to Love God, Love People, and Make Disciples. This mission is our pillar of cloud by day and our pillar of fire by night.

Vision Statement: We have an incentive to connect with Christ more, love People more, and change lives. We seek to connect with God more, and we want more people to connect with Him. We strive to love people more, and we want more people to experience His love. We want our lives to transform more, and we want to see more lives transformed.

Both read differently from my church, but all three consist of three components, *God, us (or we),* and *others*. Together, the three create a triad, i.e., a group of three closely related things. I would say that is the case in all three of these Mission Statements. It may interest you to know that I didn't have to search through many Mission Statements to find three that agreed. The two statements quoted above are from the first two websites I visited. Granted, I did visit websites for churches I trusted. Some churches call them Mission Statements; others call them Vision Statements, yet others distinguish between them and have one each. While there is a difference, some Vision Statements will read like Mission Statements. To avoid getting bogged down in semantics, I'm going to consider them synonymous. For the sake of discussion, I will refer to them collectively as Mission Statements.

It is logical and necessary that a church express its Mission Statement as a triad if you think about it. As indicated above, it is hard to instill Christ-like qualities apart from community. That is, *we* serve as the vehicle for *God* to implant Christ-like attributes in *others*. Based on my small sample of Mission Statements, I think it's safe to say that any church <u>after God's own heart</u> will have a Mission Statement expressed as a triad. I underlined "after God's own heart" for obvious reasons. I can't speak for churches that are more aligned with secular or worldly values than with God. Complexity aside, the Mission Statement is likely viewed as *the purpose statement* for the associated ministry or church.

I want to revisit the hierarchal comment I made regarding my church's Mission Statement. When presented above, I first noted that it conveyed purpose as the singular objective to make disciples, a concept simple to grasp. However, transitioning from that one endpoint to a triad elevates the Mission Statement to greater complexity. That led us to question whether there is a hierarchy among the three components. If so, what is it? In context with this hierarchy, is there a dynamic relationship to which we need to pay attention? For example, when I paraphrased my church's expanded Mission Statement, I could have said we instill Christ-like qualities in others. But that would have been an incorrect dynamic. We have no power or ability to impart anything even akin to Christ-like qualities; only God can do that. So, the correct dynamic is to *submit* ourselves to God and function *as His tool* to instill Christ-like attributes in others.

With this new wrinkle of complexity introduced into the Mission Statement, let's ask our question again. What is the central aim expressed by each of the three Mission Statements above? As I said above, do the three elements – God, us, others – serve as different components comprising purpose? Or is there one purpose that all three collectively serve to accomplish? Perhaps my church has a short version of our Mission Statement because our objective isn't that complicated. Maybe it's just to make disciples, despite the complexities introduced in the expanded version. Perhaps the purpose expressed in all three Mission Statements is simply *to make disciples.*

What We Don't See – In our discussion thus far, discipleship is the part of the iceberg that floats above the water. At our vantage point of 30,000 ft., we don't see what is floating below the water. That's the part supporting the fraction above the water and can be attributed primarily to God and us, i.e., God's instrument for discipleship.

Up to this point, I've confined the thought process to a formal Mission Statement. Implicit in the discussion was the assumption of a mutual but intuitive understanding of the meaning of "purpose." In other words, I didn't start with a formal definition. Nor did I try to establish common ground in our perception of a more abstract concept of purpose. The commonality I framed was very restrictive - the contents of a Mission Statement. While we may have common ground in the Mission Statement, we might have completely divergent opinions on a more abstract understanding of purpose. That is something we wouldn't have known. Additionally, I presented purpose as a singular goal but with multiple components necessary to achieve that goal. Considered from a hierarchal perspective, making disciples would be our only goal; God and us would be the vehicles for achieving that goal.

Let's take it to a deeper level. Let's give the idea of purpose a further twist. If I ask you your church's purpose *in implementing* a new ministry, that is not the same as your ministry's purpose. It now becomes a little more abstract because that question has no concrete answer. Making disciples is one thing; our purpose in making disciples is altogether different. That brings us to the next level of complexity in our mirror maze. Is there a singular underlying sense of meaning that gives rise to the purpose expressed in our Mission Statement? Is there an underlying objective distinct from the stated purpose of discipleship but yet permeates the Mission Statements? I suspect that no one volitionally differentiates between the stated purpose and some underlying abstract purpose. I doubt anyone sits down and deliberates how to weave a profound sense of meaning into a Mission Statement.

That requires a closer look at the idea of purpose. I won't patronize you with Webster's definition; however, I want to draw out three terms I picked out by comparing various online dictionaries. They are *reason*, *intent*, and *objective*.

1. The *reason* why we do something,
2. our *intention* in pursuing that something, and
3. the end *objective*, which we can understand as "that something."

Our initial understanding of purpose was one defined by a single (albeit multicomponent) goal. With this expanded perspective, we now understand it as multifaceted, defined by objective, reason, and intent.

Don't confuse the multi-component concept presented above with the multifaceted concept presented here. The former relates to how the three components converge onto a singular goal. The latter goes beyond objective to encompass motivation. In our bird's eye view, we understood purpose by what we could see, i.e., the tip of the iceberg. Here is where it gets a little tricky because reason and intent are as much a part of the iceberg below the water as God and us. As we plunge beneath the surface to get a closer view, we will see what gives rise to that part of the iceberg above the water. When I asked for your church's purpose in pursuing your ministry, I asked for their reason, their intent. There may be shades of difference, but I don't want to get into the weeds by trying to differentiate between the two. Instead, I will treat the two terms as synonymous and use them interchangeably or together, depending on the context.

To summarize, purpose, by application, is multicomponent like a piece of machinery with moving parts. It includes a triad of participants necessary to bring it about – God, us, and others. By definition, it is like a cut gemstone with several facets. Those facets comprise objective, reason, and intent. The objective is the end goal; reason and intent are the motivation for pursuing that end goal. The end goal <u>alone</u> is not our purpose but is necessary to give it life. Our drive to attain our goal cannot be construed as our purpose but is essential to bring it to fruition. Reason and intent need the objective and vice versa.

Membership Focus: - *I used my church's Mission Statement as a case study for an in-depth analysis of what comprises a Mission Statement. I essentially dismantled it and reassembled it so that you can see the inner workings of <u>purpose.</u> Insofar as your new ministry initiative, I would encourage you to craft your Mission Statement accordingly. Incorporate the same three components and the same three facets. So, by application, your new ministry's objective would equate to your new ministry's successful fruition, and <u>reason</u> or <u>intent</u> would equate to the motivation for pursuing the ministry.*

Noah's Perspective – Let's bring in our host at this point. What was Noah's sense of purpose? What was his motivation; what was his objective? The Bible doesn't say; it just reads (in so many words), "You shall…." To all appearances, whatever personal reason Noah might have had was irrelevant. So, did I just destroy my entire discussion on purpose in one fell swoop? No, there is more to come. We don't need the Bible to tell us he had a reason. We can see meaning in his actions without knowing that reason. What was his purpose? Note, I'm talking about Noah, not God.

Let's put on our secular hat and say Noah's default motivation was to save his own skin and that of his family. Does that mean saving humanity or civilization was more a benefit than a reason? Or is the latter an extension of the former and, therefore, the same? We can only surmise what Noah might have been thinking.

And what of the animal kingdom? His goal seemingly was to save eight people, but he builds an Ark big enough to accommodate a city. As absurd as it sounds, one could argue that the real motivation for constructing the Ark was to save the animal kingdom. And God let eight people tag along since someone needed to take care of the animals anyway. Don't laugh; anyone to whom Romans 1:18-25 applies would embrace this reason. So why did he build it so big if not for the animals? The animals are subject to man; man is not subject to the animals. Yes, God specified a boat large enough to save the animal kingdom, but only to serve as part of Noah's infrastructure after the flood.

And then there is the aspect of evangelizing his world? Did God have a Plan B in which He sized the Ark to carry all the people who would have repented if they had repented? But Genesis doesn't even mention Noah preaching to the population; we only know that from New Testament scripture. Try and develop a Mission Statement from all these considerations. Left to our imagination, it all becomes very complicated and speculative.

Why? – Our discussion on the multifaceted nature of purpose has been somewhat ambiguous up to this point. Let's get a little more specific. Earlier I asked whether a singular underlying sense of meaning gives rise to our stated purpose, which I later identified as reason or intent. Let me ask that again in light of our more comprehensive understanding of purpose. Reread the Mission Statements above or read your church's statement and see if you can see reason or intent embedded in them. Would you say that request is a little vague? I would. So, let's downshift and bring it to a more fundamental level, that of a child's perspective. Sometimes that gives us more clarity of thought than trying to get philosophical as an adult. Here goes, *Why are we pursuing the new ministry?* Yes, it is that simple. It is that childlike. The answer to that question is the majority of the iceberg below the water. It is the *foundational basis* of the end goal we are declaring in our Mission Statement. That foundational basis is our mooring point, our reference point.

    Here is where I'm going to get myself in serious trouble. I didn't expect you to find reason or intent in those statements because I couldn't. In my church's case, nowhere in our Mission Statement is a motive for why we are trying to make disciples. In looking at the other Mission Statements presented, I can't see reason in those either. Does that make them inferior statements? Not at all. Each of them hits the bullseye in its unique way, but none of them conveys why that church is pursuing its end goal. So, while we can probably agree that Mission and Vision Statements clearly express the objective, I'm not sure the authors <u>designed</u> them to provide reason or intent. I'm not sure we can establish the *"why"* based strictly on the statement's wording. Should that worry us? It should if we don't know the basis for the Mission Statement. How do we know it is of God and not the ambition of a pastor or church leader? This ambiguous understanding hearkens back to my comment that yours and my sense of purpose may be utterly divergent at the abstract level, and we wouldn't know it. That is because most of us have little more than a subjective, abstract perception of what purpose means.

I will say that there is a definitive underlying driver. We have talked about it in generalities but haven't defined it, so it wasn't a pointless assignment. Having not been present at any planning meetings, I won't speculate on the inspirations behind any of the Mission Statements we've reviewed. Also, I won't guess as to possible motivations why any church might want to pursue a ministry initiative. While we are navigating our wooded terrain, I would ask you to contemplate these things, and then we will compare notes later.

What is Your Mooring Point? – Part of the problem is that our Mission Statements, by their very nature, are restrictive. They need to be simple to be understood. If we increase their complexity to make them less constrictive, then they become unwieldy. When we confine our attention to the Mission Statement, we limit our understanding of what purpose means. Without any broader framework, the Mission Statement becomes the box to which our thinking is confined. Without that framework, we are not able to think outside of the box. However, by bringing in the ideas of reason and intent, we essentially challenge why the box exists in the first place. In effect, we cast off the restraints placed on the Mission Statement itself.

That last statement generated a curious sensation in me. I had a feeling of being lost at sea. As long as I remained within the confines of my Mission Statement, I felt secure. Yet, when I questioned the very basis of that Mission Statement, I lost that security. I felt like I was floating in a vast open ocean with no horizontal or vertical reference points. I had no mooring point and no tether on which to hang. I can only surmise that I felt that way because I realized at the moment that my mooring point had been the *objective* expressed in the Mission Statement. In reality, my mooring point should be the underlying *justification,* <u>not the end goal</u>. The foundational basis for the Mission Statement may be abstract, but it is a reality. If we can't identify that justification, how do we know our mission is legitimate?

When I noted that the starting point for many is a formalized Mission Statement, I would submit that the beginning starts before that, with an informal understanding of reason or intent. That said, we can significantly benefit if we come to grips with our motivation before we write the Mission Statement. It's our tether, our mooring point. Understanding the objective but not the inspiration imparts a measure of vagueness to our sense of meaning. I compare it to waking up on a train and being informed of where you are headed but not why you are going there or why you left in the first place.

What it Means at the Corporate Level – Realistically, little of what I talked about is at the forefront of conversation in our efforts to launch new ministries. That's why I'm bringing it up here. When I said a sense of purpose begins with a formal written statement like a Mission Statement or a Vision Statement, I skipped over how these statements come about. They generally aren't drafted up by the staff or in church business meetings but by committees. To expedite the planning process, the church body or leadership selects a committee from the church body at large. The committee then functions as the surrogate for the membership. In that capacity, they do the heavy lifting insofar as planning and strategizing.

Those who have not had the privilege of serving on a committee should understand that the committee members will always have a greater awareness of purpose than the membership. The committee

Life Event Number 2 - Noah

lives and breathes the ministry's details until they present it to the congregation for a vote. On the other hand, the church membership has little or no idea of what's going on and comes into the presentation cold. They rely on the committee spokesperson to explain the "whys" and "wherefores" of how the committee arrived at the end product and its Mission Statement. The chief concern here is that the committee presentation may focus on the weightier matters of strategy and logistics and not the simple "*why*," which is essential for understanding.

In addressing the corporate level, I am speaking of the membership partly as a collective and partly as a group of individuals with independent opinions and perceptions. As a collective, there is a collective opinion or perception that characterizes the membership as a body. The more influential individuals typically form the views and perceptions of the whole. So, the collective moves together as a unit because the vast majority of the members want to do what everyone else is doing or what *they think* everyone else wants. It's similar to cultural posturing when people of different nationalities get together for a social event. Out of respect for Culture-A, a person from Culture-B does things they think are Culture-A customs. On the other hand, the person from Culture-A is unfamiliar with these actions but responds in like kind because they believe it's a Culture-B custom.

When it comes to a Mission Statement's contents or meaning, the membership generally takes its cues from the committee charged with ministry development. While this is a necessary approach, it does have its disadvantages. Chiefly we, the membership collective, cease to think for ourselves, and we readily accept the committee's rendition of Mission. The present-day term for that is "group think." In that capacity, individuals adopt without question the message the church body has been encouraged to adopt. To our discredit, that's how we prefer it because as insensitive as it sounds, we consider it the committee's job to do our thinking for us.

For example, in my church's Mission Statement, did any of the members even question the simplicity of that statement? Did anyone comment that it's too simple? Or did anyone think the target objective should be evangelism or having a deeper walk with Christ – themes and variations on discipleship, but not the same. By contrast, did members of the churches that developed the other two statements comment that their Mission Statements were too complicated? Probably not because all of them sound good. Why would anyone question them and dissect them when "smarter" people worked long nights on the details of the ministry initiative.

Above all, did anyone ask *why* we are pursuing these ministries? Again, probably not because this is where the reason gets lost in the shuffle. By the time the committee develops the Mission Statement, we are way past the *"why."* I'm reasonably sure that if anyone asked that question at this point in the process, 1. The committee spokesperson would be caught totally off guard and be speechless, and 2. Everyone would turn and stare at the person as though to say, what kind of question is that? That's why we don't ask simple but probing questions like that.

Unless you have had previous experience in such endeavors or have other church statements as templates, you generally don't question what you don't see. For simple Mission Statements, you don't see the potential benefit of greater complexity. For complex statements, you don't see the potential value that less is more. You don't know what the committee considered and discarded, i.e., different phraseologies that gave nuances of meaning that may have been undesirable or misleading. And, of course, you probably don't see reason or intent embedded in the statement.

It's not that we are discouraged or even prohibited from questioning the message. It's the idea that the committee has put a lot more thought into developing the message than the rank and file member. Because of this, we feel we are at a disadvantage and don't question the Mission Statement.

My point is not to have you find fault with the goal of your Mission Statement. My point is to encourage you to focus on the reason and intent - the foundational basis for your mission or vision. Focus on it from the beginning, and don't lose sight of it as the ministry's launch recedes in the rearview mirror. It's conceivable that we become so fixated on our objective that the reason for our ministry is more of a formality than a foundational principle.

It may also be that the church leadership explained the reason with great clarity. Yet, it came across as usual church rhetoric, at which point, everyone's eyes glazed over. From the opposite side of the podium, the rank and file member may not consider the reason to be an issue because of our inherent trust in our leadership to hear from God and act accordingly. If you were to poll the membership regarding the "why," what kind of answers would you get? I venture to say that a high percentage of people would answer with a paraphrased version of the Mission Statement. Their response would sound more like the end goal than why your church is pursuing that goal. I would also venture to say that many would be honest enough to say they don't know. But there are always a precious few who do know the right reason. Put yourself in this situation and ask yourself if the motivation was misguided, would you know it?

Membership Focus: - *Most of us are not involved in deciding whether to pursue a new ministry. If you are one of these, are you willing to take it on faith that your church is pursuing this ministry for the right reason?*

So why split hairs over something so fundamental as the question of *why*? I intend to demonstrate a correct *"why"* and an incorrect *"why."* I expect to show a right *motivation* and a wrong motivation. How can our drive for pursuing a legitimate ministry need be amiss? If it is incompatible with God's motive, it is wrong. The two do not have to be the same, only compatible. I will touch on the difference later.

For example, suppose the mission serves the physical needs of an unchurched subgroup within the community (period). Again, why are we doing it? Are we doing this to put our church on the map? Is it to get "those people" to darken our doors? Is it to set up our church as a beacon of community service? My next question is, why do we want to become a beacon of community service? Why do we want to get "those people" to darken our doors? I think our iceberg just melted because it's starting to get a little warm in here. As noble as these reasons sound, they are all wrong motives. They are not bad results, but they are the wrong reasons. Recall our discussion about flesh-driven churches. It has everything to do with that.

Again, our reason serves as the foundation of the objective. Accordingly, we should interweave it into the Mission Statement. I will go so far as to say that the *"why"* is more important as the guiding light for the ministry initiative than the objective. Going back to the Mission Statement of my church, did you notice how simple it is? It easily lends itself as a guiding light or a guiding principle for our church. But again, why are we doing it? Here is the critical point: it doesn't matter what the goal is or how noble it is if the *"why"* of ministry implementation and participation is wrong. Therefore, it is critically important that we not only understand the message, i.e., the ministry objective and target audience, but the underpinnings of that message, i.e., the "why."

What it Means at the Individual Level – This section deals with members as distinct from the collective. Can we draw a distinction between reason/intent at the corporate level and the same at the individual level? Why does the individual get involved in a ministry? Let's delve into some homebrewed motives individual church members might express. As noted above, any given layperson might paraphrase the Mission Statement as the perceived reason they are involved. Yet, their unspoken motive might be unrelated. Here are some personal reasons people might use to get involved in ministries.

- It makes me feel so uplifted and close to God,
- I immerse myself in this ministry to get away from my problems,
- They recruited me because of my position at this church,
- I want to be on the ground floor of something big,
- I just love the sense of shared excitement in this new ministry; and,
- The pastor's inspiration and passion are catching and have set the membership on fire (which, by the way, isn't a wrong motive. That's kind of what pastors are for – to lead*)*.

While these motives may not coincide with the ministry's real reason, they don't necessarily conflict with it. Because of that, they may or may not be legitimate. We will revisit these later.

Membership Focus: *In transitioning from corporate buy-in to individual buy-in, let's make it more personal. Besides your role as a prayer warrior, what is **your** motive for participating in your new ministry?*

As noted above, most church members may see little or no distinction between objective and reason. For most, it's just not an issue. I would venture to say that most don't think it's crucial to their ministry involvement. That goes back to the idea that the rank and file members typically have an innate faith in the church leadership and their judgment on why their church is pursuing the ministry. In other words, we who are the rank and file are just foot soldiers doing what the leadership tells us to do. Do I think the rank and file members should know the difference between reason and objective? I do. It would escalate their zeal for service, and it would benefit the overall image of their church. It would be a simple thing to educate ministry participants on why they are pursuing a ministry initiative. Now, will this capture all the individuals comprising the membership? Probably not. It depends on each individual's spiritual maturity and understanding of their calling, i.e., whether they are even aware God has called them. However, it will capture those who know God has called them and who need to understand the base motivation.

Membership Focus: *Right now, you may be questioning the "why" of a ministry initiative. Many in your membership are likely unaware of the "why" but haven't voiced it or thought of it. To effectively pray for your fellow church members, can you understand why you must grasp the ministry's <u>core</u> reason?*

Crafting the Statement - Now, let's touch on the attention given to the Mission Statement's creation. That has to do with all facets of purpose, not just reason and intent, and we achieve it by asking the following four questions.

1. Is the formal effort of crafting the statement preceded by a meaningful prayer effort?
2. Is there a significant amount of discussion and thought invested in developing the document?
3. Is the mission statement's actual intent to serve as a guiding light or guiding principle for the Ministry?
4. Does the Mission Statement serve as the basis for planning and designing the ministry strategy?

Now ask these questions from the heart, not the head, because no one involved in ministry planning will answer "no" to any of the four, but what do their actions show. What does their day-to-day conversation reveal? People always blow their cover in their casual conversation. My concern with these questions is that the mission statement may be relegated to an administrative checkbox because mission strategy is the primary focus. Its spoken reason is to serve as the guiding principle of the ministry. Yet, its actual function may be nothing more than window dressing to give it a professional polish. Why does that matter as long as the mission strategy doesn't conflict with the Mission Statement? It matters because nothing will keep the mission objective from deviating from the intended pathway should fleshly influences infiltrate the ministry. As asked, the four questions above were essentially one-sided. We should ask them as follows:

1. Does a meaningful prayer effort precede the physical action, or does the prayer effort consist only of the obligatory opening prayer at each committee meeting?

2. Is there a significant level of effort invested in developing the Mission Statement, or is it treated as no more than the necessary "paperwork" for the ministry?

3. Is the Mission Statement a perpetual guiding light for the ministry, or is it stuffed into a filing cabinet to be out of sight, out of mind?

4. Is the Mission Statement the basis for planning and designing the ministry strategy, or does planning operate on a parallel but independent path from the Mission Statement?

Here are a couple of litmus tests that will help you discern whether the Mission Statement is actually held in deference or is merely window dressing.

1. Before now, were you even aware of a Mission Statement for your church or any ministry under its banner?

2. How often is the Mission Statement dusted off and used as a measuring stick or plumb line to determine whether the ministry is on track as originally planned?

Mission and vision may be touted as indispensable elements of every ministry initiative but do they live up to their reputation? Are they promoted as the central theme to ministry execution? Churches may create formal Mission Statements to define the ministry on paper, but how often do these statements function as the ministry's guiding principle? Does every aspect of the ministry initiative from inception to maturity exude meaning aligned with the Mission Statement's objective? I include reason and intent in this idea of meaning.

Right now, let's bring our host Noah back into the discussion and demonstrate how easy it might be to get off track.

Life Event Number 2 - Noah

It would have been easy for Noah to have gotten sidetracked by taking personal responsibility for gathering the animals or the best approach for preaching to his community. If you read the Genesis account carefully, it appears that Noah didn't lift a finger to fetch the animals. Genesis 7:8 says, *Pairs of clean and unclean animals...**came to** Noah and entered the ark (NIV)*. I interpret that to mean he didn't go out and find them; that would have been a hoot watching him round up a bunch of monkeys. If Noah took personal responsibility to fetch the animals, he would have worked at cross purposes with God. Then there might have been two sets of animals. At the risk of throwing away everything I've said up to this point, I'm convinced that the purpose God has appointed to us is not so complicated as to require a purpose statement. We just create them to make sure everyone is on the same page and to look organized.

Let's Take a Detour - Now, let's address the other side issue before it gets too far in the rearview mirror. How did Noah's preaching ministry fit into the grand scheme of things – especially as it applies to the purpose of your church's core ministry. While Noah preached to his neighbors, that wasn't Plan B, and it was not his purpose; it was a byproduct. Undoubtedly, God didn't want to deny the inhabitants of the earth the opportunity to repent. Still, I doubt whether God expected it. He wouldn't have released Noah to build the Ark if evangelism was a viable option. Why would God assign a lengthy, arduous task if there were even a low probability it would be in vain? The answer is He wouldn't; God doesn't need backup plans.

How would it look if Noah got to the finishing touches and God said, "Noah, you are such a skilled orator at evangelizing the world we won't need the Ark, after all. Convert it to a theme park." I have

Life Event Number 2 - Noah

my doubts as to whether God even suggested that he preach to his neighbors, but I don't think He told him not to. Noah's preaching ministry was just a natural consequence of undertaking a bazaar construction project. There would be no lack of spectators asking questions. I can imagine his first encounter went like this:

Neighbor: "Hey Noah, whatcha doin'?"

Noah: "I'm building (scrape, scrape) a really big boat (scrape, scrape) to save my family... (scrape, scrape, scrape, scrape) ...

(pause for a breath) .... and as many animals as I can pack into it."

Neighbor (long pause): "Do what?"

Noah (laying down his adze): "Look, all I know is that God told me He is going to wipe out civilization with a giant flood. And he instructed me to build this Ark for my family and me to survive. So, if you want to get on board, the conditions are that you repent of your evil deeds and, um, offer sacrifices to God. I think that's all. I don't believe there are any other conditions. Oh, and friends and family? They have to repent on their own.

They can't come in on the coattails of your repentance." (picks up adze and resumes work)

Neighbor: Stunned silence.

And in follow-up segments to this conversation, I'm sure Noah realized the need to polish his presentation so it didn't sound so incredulous and had the feel of an actual sermon.

If Noah's God-given purpose had been to evangelize the world, it would have happened just because God is sovereign. He would have accomplished that objective through Noah just like He accomplished the salvation of Nineveh through Jonah – both unlikely scenarios. Our problem is that we impose our sense of the *unlikely* and the *impossible* onto God. That has a direct bearing on how to pray for our church. Noah failed in evangelizing the world because that wasn't his God-given purpose.

And Chase a Rabbit - Now let me catch a rabbit here before it gets away. As presented, one could mistakenly understand that God in His sovereignty could have saved the antediluvian civilization. Yet, for some reason, He didn't. Some would love to jump on that as evidence that there is no compassion from God. Let me compare that civilization to fresh fruit and vegetables. With some modifications, this principle can be extended to Christians as well. Freshly picked and in our prime, we are serviceable for the Master's purpose. But if we choose not to let God use us and decide to walk along the path of the flesh, our series of choices cause us to become less and less fresh. Up to a point, we are still salvageable and are still functional, but like fruit and vegetables, at some point, we spoil and cannot be salvaged for service.

Don't confuse this analogy of spoiled fruit with losing your salvation. For Christians, the comparison would apply to our role in the church, not salvation. Consider the following plausible scenario. God calls someone at age 20 to a specific ministry, such as child evangelism. However, that someone resists up until the age of 50, at which point she surrenders. Realistically, at this point, she only has a useful life of maybe 10 to 20 years versus 40 to 50 years, had she submitted when God first called her. Sure, God can use her, but will He extend her life to restore her lost years? Not likely, but that would be His call. Taking this scenario to its logical conclusion, what would happen if the woman waited until she was

65 before surrendering to that ministry? I began child evangelism when I was 15, but the scenario painted above could have been me. Noah's purpose was not to evangelize the ancient world because they had spoiled themselves through the series of flesh-driven choices they made.

Membership Focus: *The take-away from this discussion is to not confuse your purpose with issues that may be good and noble but are peripheral. If pursued, these peripheral issues would distract from your appointed purpose. If Noah had suspended work to travel the known world and preach until people repented, he would have missed the boat – literally.*

Summary - Let's pause and take stock of where we are and where we are going because we are most of the way through the woods. I initially presented purpose as an objective. That represented the dense, wooded terrain – simple in concept but broad, vague, and ill-defined. It was easy to lose your bearing. I then expanded it to a multi-component model. Without further inquiry, that advanced concept was considered completely satisfactory in conveying a complete understanding of purpose. We then pulled back the curtains to discover more than meets the eye by introducing the other components of reason and intent. We expanded the concept to go beyond the objective by probing its underlying basis. We questioned the ministry's "why." Despite the lack of a clear trail, the woods are becoming less intimidating because we have climbed in elevation. The underbrush is thinning, making it easier to navigate. We can look down and see where we have been and where we need to go. We now have a more comprehensive understanding. We have come to realize that there is more to our purpose than just a Mission Statement.

In the discussion thus far, I also presented the concept of purpose as a dynamic relationship between the end goal and the supporting motivation for pursuing that goal. When I say "supporting motivation," I don't want to relegate that to be subordinate to the end goal. I felt like I was definitive in characterizing the objective. Yet, I was deliberately broad and vague in portraying reason and intent. In doing so, I may have communicated that reason is ministry specific or church specific. You may have come away with the impression that I didn't identify particular motivations because they are ministry-specific. I may have conveyed the idea that one size <u>does not</u> fit all. What may be the right motivation for your new ministry initiative may not be the right motivation for a ministry with a different goal.

That would imply that the underlying meaning built into a Mission statement could take on any number of pathways depending on the ministry's scope and target population. In taking the ill-defined path, I wanted to prompt a realization that the average church member probably has an erroneous understanding of purpose. I intended to show that the average church member is quite content to amble through church life, blissfully ignorant of why we do what we do. Hopefully, this same exercise had the benefit of whetting your curiosity and stimulating your creative juices to speculate on what this cryptic driver could be for your church ministries. The path I took us along is what it's like to look through a glass darkly. As promised, I will now provide the answer that is *very simple conceptually* but not simple.

But then Face to Face

Uniform Simplicity - In actuality, I don't believe reason and intent change according to the ministry objective. I do think that one size *does* fit all. In giving you the straight answer, I already gave it away twice. You may have noticed and wondered why I ran past it without drawing attention to it. Or perhaps you thought I was so fixated on making some convoluted argument that I was unaware of the simple truth. Following are excerpts of the two times I gave it away.

Introduction to Noah (2nd ¶):

"We do know that anyone undertaking such a monumental task would have to be unequivocally certain that God called him to do so."

The section entitled "What It Means at the Corporate Level" (10th paragraph):

"... the rank and file member may not consider the reason to be an issue because of our inherent trust in our leadership to hear from God and act accordingly."

In discussing Noah, would it be legitimate to dispense with the speculative points and say his master purpose, his core sense of meaning, was **just to obey God**? As implied in the introduction, that in and of itself should be sufficient. That, in and of itself, would be the most straightforward, uncomplicated motivation. That eliminates all arguable nuances associated with building the Ark. By extension, that removes all arguable nuances associated with any ministry initiative we may take on. That, in and of itself, is looking **face to face**. What do the two statements quoted above declare insofar as reason and intent? They affirm obedience to God – period end of discussion! The very act of accepting the mission objective is our act of obedience.

So, is that all there is to it? Is it that simple? It is that simple.

I would say we've come out of the woods and reached the pinnacle of the mountain we've been climbing. Relax, take a rest. Spread out your arms and breathe deeply. Take in the cool breeze, warm sunshine, and the vast expanse below. Find rest in the realization that if you knew nothing more than to hear God tell you to start walking, you would not need to know anything else. Why am I walking, you ask? I'm walking because God told me to; that's all I need to know. Knowledge of my destination is not required because my God is sufficient. But we're getting ahead of ourselves; that's a story for Abraham.

Compatibility Within Conflict

- On the trip down the mountain, let's return to the discussion of potentially conflicting purposes. Noah has more to teach us here. After that, we will finish our trek with the application of what it all means.

Resuming our discussion, if you were to say Noah's sole purpose was to obey God, my "sense of duty" would say you are right. Here is where it gets complicated. I questioned earlier whether a sense of responsibility to obey God was sufficient motivation for Noah to see it through to the end. My understanding of how the flesh operates would say you would be dead wrong – his sense of responsibility is not sufficient to see it through to the end. At what point does the flesh burn out on doing what is right - in this case, staying on course to finish the ark? At what point does Noah's sense of duty wear thin? To say that Noah's sense of duty is sufficient motivation assumes that his sense of responsibility can overcome his inherent self-serving drive. I do not use the word "inherent" here lightly. Our propensity to be self-serving is innate, i.e., inherited. In spiritual parlance, relying solely on his sense of duty would translate into the assumption that Noah's spiritual dimension can dominate the fleshly aspect indefinitely. Again, knowing humanity the way I do, I am confident that's not the case. So, how do we reconcile this? In the following discussion, I'm going to peel back several layers on our onion.

Most people are sharp enough to understand that multiple goals can coexist in a single endeavor. There has to be a hierarchy in such a scenario, and only one can be the *Master Purpose.* All others are *subordinate* or *intermediate objectives.* Considered independently, all the endpoints in a series of endpoints compete for dominance, thereby setting up a conflictual relationship. That brings to bear the dynamic relationship between reason, intent, and objective. It also elicits a consideration of the dynamic relationship of multiple goals. So, you wouldn't be wrong to say his purpose in the immediate was to obey God, in the intermediate to save him and his family, and in the long term to save civilization. The latter two cannot be his purpose, but of necessity, become goals subordinate to his purpose.

Taken independently, these can easily compete with one another, depending on the number of participants that might champion each endpoint. Taken as a hierarchy, these align so they are not incompatible or conflicting goals. Nor are they mutually exclusive objectives. In this vein, we can say it was a symbiotic relationship between Noah and God. Both parties benefit. As a side note, one could argue that Noah's motive and objective are the same from a flesh-driven perspective. For example, what is your goal, Noah? It is to save my family and humanity. Why are you doing this, Noah? To salvage my family and my descendants who will repopulate the earth, i.e., civilization.

Membership Focus: *Let me ask you a loaded question. Do you need a reason to launch a new ministry initiative?*

I'll admit that I was a little disingenuous in asking this question the way I did. What I meant was, do you need a personal reason to launch or participate in a new ministry initiative? Should it not come down to the most fundamental motivator to just obey God?

Introducing the personal dimension brings us to the next layer of our onion.

It's Personal. Ok. - Let's loop back to our definition of purpose for a moment. I'm not sure why, but couching "purpose" in terms of words like "reason" and "intent" is impersonal. I see the idea of "objective" as cold and calculating. I can have reason and intent without my end goal having value or worth. For example, let's suppose that Noah's ulterior motive was to salvage as much worldly wealth as he could. What value would that have since after the Flood, he owned the whole world anyway and had nowhere to spend his money?

Craig Groeschel, the author of the book Chazown (2010), describes how to find God's purpose for your personal life. He makes two very strategic observations.

1. Many Christians never arrive at any definite conclusion regarding God's purpose for their lives and
2. Few people in life find out "their purpose <u>on purpose</u>." It does not occur by accident.

Neither will your church discover theirs by accident. What can we infer from these statements? If your church is content managing the status quo, God probably won't reveal His purpose. In commenting on this idea, please don't be lulled into the false belief that God's will for your church is to manage the status quo.

Another observation Craig makes is critical to the whole process of finding our purpose. "<u>You must be desperate to honor God with Your life</u>" (Groeschel, 2010). That really should give us some insight on how to pray to this end.

In context with Craig's observations, I want to introduce a more profound component only implied in the definition of purpose. That component is to "justify our existence." That makes it personal because it brings me personally into the equation. It shifts the emphasis from the impersonal *we*, the church, to *me*, an integral part of the church. It means I have skin in the game. If I view it as *we*, then I and everyone else involved can engage in the proverbial circular firing squad if the ministry initiative fails. If, on the other hand, the responsibility rests on *me*, then it comes back on me if the ministry initiative fails. So, in reevaluating purpose in context with this new component, let me clarify. I'm treating the idea of *justifying our existence* as the subjective *visceral motivation* for achieving my goal and *reason* or *intent* as the *"sense of duty" motivation* for achieving that same objective. Justifying our existence or our justification gives us better focus when we pray for the church.

Lanes Merging – Blend with the Flow - Let's re-ask our initial question of Noah in light of our discussion to this point. What was his *justification*, and what was his *reason* or *intent*? Thus far, based on our analysis, I can equate his reason or intent with his "sense of duty," i.e., to obey God. That would be in line with the idea of "being desperate to honor God." However, I am struggling to accept the belief that we honor God out of a sense of duty in contrast to a visceral, emotional response. I wrestle with it because I know the counter viewpoint that we honor God out of gratitude for what He has done for us. I lean toward the former simply because our emotions are fickle.

I will touch on the alternative perspective later but stay with me on how we honor God out of a sense of responsibility. In this regard, we will take Noah's intent as his Master Purpose – the "sense of duty" component. Relating this to whether you need a reason to be involved in a ministry initiative, the answer is Yes? It is "to honor God." That's all. For Noah, that would relegate the idea of saving his family to justifying his existence – i.e., skin in the game or the visceral component.

Finally, I need to bring in a critical factor without which the previous discussion is all for naught. We can view responsibility and justification as reactive as opposed to proactive. Further, one can construe the latter as avoiding loss, i.e., I stand to lose something if I don't do it. Regarding the component of duty, one can construe it as a chore, i.e., we are doing it because we must. Is there no component of purpose that involves the *desire* to do it? Case in point, how often do you engage in recreation because you must, not because you want to? Or closer to home, you go to work because you have to. But if you don't enjoy your occupation, how long is that going to last? That is where we come full circle with the scripture passage for Guideline #2. *And we know that all things work together for good to those who love God, to those who are the called according to His purpose* (Romans 8:28). Another New Testament passage that supplements the Romans passage is John 14: 21-24. That is the passage where Jesus lays down the binary principle: *If anyone loves Me, he will keep My word.... He who does not love Me does not keep My words.* There is no third door. My question is, to what degree did Noah's love for God instill in him the drive necessary to endure to the end.

Membership Focus: *How much does your passion for God instill in you the drive to endure the hardships, setbacks, and discouragements inherent in a ministry? As I will touch on later, does your passion for God reduce these setbacks to common nuisances?*

We must anchor our *objective motivation* and *visceral motivation* in our ~~gratitude~~ passion for God if we expect our sense of purpose to endure hardships. That has everything to do with your reason for participating in a ministry initiative, not your church's corporate reason. However, the latter is equally important because your reason needs to align with the corporate purpose. If some members are going along for the ride and have not taken ownership of the corporate purpose or don't know what drives their own sense of meaning, are they contributing anything?

In that context, let's revisit the question of, "Why am I doing this?" Except let's go one level deeper and take it to the visceral level. Why is it worth my time and effort to do this? Have you ever stopped short in the middle of a frustrating, labor-intensive task and asked yourself, "why in the world am I doing this?" That is the frame of mind you should ask yourself the same question regarding any ministry initiative your church may be involved in or contemplating. The reason may surprise you. Doing it just because it makes us feel good or feel spiritual is not *justifying* our existence. Some of the motives enumerated above are fine and good. I wouldn't deny anyone those experiences, but they are not drivers. They can be exhilarating, and they add color and variety to our lives. Still, they carry a retail store newness that wears off with time and becomes routine and mundane. In short, these experiences are not founded on ~~gratitude~~ a passion for God but on a sense of "I'm bored, what can I do that is new and different?"

Human logic would say Noah's core reason for building the Ark was to save him and his family first and foremost and secondarily obey God. For the average person, the visceral *motivation* for saving his family would be the Master Reason, and obeying God would be a convenient excuse for prioritizing the visceral motivation. However, keep in mind the average person died in the Flood.

No! Noah placed his love and respect for God above his passion for life; that makes the visceral component take a back seat. That brings the Romans and John passages in as principle supporting pillars of our argument. One may assert that I'm reading an awful lot into scripture when the Bible doesn't specifically say it? I believe it to be so because that would be a characteristic of a godly, righteous Noah that pursues after God and the *reason* God chose him. For God to have singled out Noah from the depraved culture engulfing him indicates he was desperate to honor God with his life.

Membership Focus: *Discovering God's purpose for your church parallels the discovery of God's purpose for your personal life.*

Corporately, we must be desperate to honor God with our lives. We will call that Rule #1.

Gathering Our Threads on Purpose - So, let's reconcile our discussion points as they relate to Noah. I'm going to say Noah's Master Reason was to obey God. Granted, the fact that Noah had a vested interest in obeying God might blur the lines, but I will sharpen the lines when I bring all my threads together. Also, keep in mind that God approached Noah, not vice versa. Noah only knew of the coming Flood because God told him so, not because he discovered it through climate modeling independent of God's calling. In this sense, obedience stands out as the chief motivating reason for building the Ark. Again, that eliminates a lot of speculation as to Noah's sense of purpose.

Now let's bring God into the equation. Remember when I made the point that our purpose must be compatible with God's but not necessarily the same? Until now, we have mentioned God's purpose for Noah only in passing. It appears to be simple, filter out the bad and keep the good. Let's see if we can mesh God's purpose with Noah's. That isn't just an academic exercise; there is benefit here as well.

First, let's contrast Noah's and God's reasons. As it pertains to Noah, God's reason was to salvage his creation through one family. Noah's was to obey God. We can say Noah served as God's tool to save humanity just as an adze served as Noah's tool to build the Ark. That's a vertical reconciliation of purpose called reciprocity. The two reasons are different, but they are compatible and serve one another. Now let's contrast God's justification with Noah's justification. God's was to give Noah a vested interest in His plan to *salvage His creation* – same as His reason. Noah's was to save his family and, by extension, *to preserve* civilization by building the

Life Event Number 2 - Noah

Ark. Wow! They are identical. That is a horizontal reconciliation or meshing of purposes. Taken together with the vertical component, we see *an alignment of purposes*. Do not lose sight of this.

So, what does all this mean? Ok, here is where I sharpen the lines. Here is where I give the conceptually simple answer. That is, it's simple to understand, but it's not a simple answer; it is a compound answer. It's like a coin; you can't separate the two sides. Heads: your motivation first and foremost is to obey God's calling. Tails: with this calling comes a *vested interest* in your effort to achieve the end goal. The term "vested" means you have something to lose if you don't step up to the plate, or perhaps more accurately, there is something you won't gain.

Before we move on to the application, let me close the loop and summarize. Bringing forward some crucial statements I made above,

> *would it be legitimate to dispense with the speculative points and say his master purpose, his core sense of meaning, was just to obey God?*
>
> *Is that all there is to it? Is it that simple?*

It is, and it isn't.

It is that simple in the sense that obedience to God is the Master Reason. No other reason should trump this. It isn't that simple in the sense that our fleshly failings introduce a complicating factor. We require a vested interest to motivate or carry us through to the end goal.

Of course, all this assumes an abiding love for God that imparts the enduring strength and stamina to your commitment. In my discussion on how our passion for God relates to our pursuits, I rejected the term gratitude deliberately. That is, where there was the option to use "gratitude" or "passion," I chose "passion" and struck "gratitude" for what God has done for us. I see gratitude as an unstable master. I view it as similar to happiness, a temporal quality that is dependent on circumstances. For example, when God doesn't meet expectations, does that increase your gratitude for Him? We can also view it as an addictive scenario. In that regard, we always need to be fed new miracles or new favors from God to keep our gratitude alive. Gratitude is good in its proper place, and it can be a driver, but it shouldn't be the principal driver; it should be a subordinate driver. I would say that love not only precedes obedience but that the litmus test for love is obedience.

So, where does our passion for God originate? I believe that it's part of the original equipment He endows us with when we come into this world. I think God instilled it in us at creation. It's part and parcel of being created in His image. But love only grows through an intentional walk with God devoid of expectations, unlike a quid pro quo walk with God. Going back to Adam and Eve, we can say that our passion for God has to be the master, and our pursuit of a designated goal has to be the slave.

Having pontificated on my viewpoint of the love-obedience dynamic, I recognize the camp that espouses the belief that obedience precedes love. That is, if you obey, love will follow. In that camp, we obey, God blesses us, gratitude follows, and passion grows, prompting further obedience. So, you guessed it, which came first, the chicken or the egg? As with other issues with divergent viewpoints, I don't want to hijack this conversation with an academic discussion that serves only to derail us from the call to obey. Irrespective of which camp you are in, we can probably agree that love and obedience set up a continuous feedback loop in which blessings and gratitude are integral catalysts. That is, they jump-start each other.

Bringing all my threads together, what does it all mean. We are *willing* partners *with God* as distinct from mere servants carrying out instructions. And that takes on the following special meaning:

God can do it without us, but He **won't** do it without us.

Jesus reinforced this point in John 15:15: *No longer do I call you servants, for a servant does not know what his master is doing; but I have called you friends, for all things that I heard from My Father I have made known to you.*

Author and Finisher – Since God is the author of our purpose, a natural consequence of pursuing it is to breathe life into our ministries. When we embrace that as our life's meaning, it gives us an appreciation of our partnership with God. It provides us with a perception of ownership. As partners, you are God's face to the community.

Uniqueness is a Virtue - We discussed partnering with God under Adam and Eve and revisited it here. Still, I want to solidify that concept further. Before we make some practical applications, I want to make one additional point of differentiation.

- Consistency – All churches should be cookie-cutter in purpose.

Yes! No!

Yes, we should all be consistent in our core purpose (sense of duty), but no, all churches should not be cookie-cutter in their objective.

Membership Focus: *As God has a predestined purpose and plan for all His children, He will also have one for your church.*

There's nothing quite like a church that's fired up for God and has a keen sense of purpose. They will be on a mission for God, and they will also be very aware of why they are doing it. In contemplating this, realize that no two churches are just alike. God calls each to its unique mission.

Membership Focus: *In becoming aware of this grand purpose, I counsel you to avoid a common trap. If you are taking your cues from other successful churches, you may well miss God's purpose for your church. Don't fall into the trap of "follow the leader." Third Baptist may have won accolades for their high-profile ministry. That doesn't mean you should spend lots of money so they can instruct your church on "How We Did It" and sell books you won't read so that you can do the same. Not so fast. If God wants you to be an understudy of Third Baptist and you feel He has made that clear to your leadership, then OK, go for it. Or if Third Baptist's ministry is more general, like updated approaches for ministering to specific target groups, then make it happen. If, on the other hand, you think God wants you to imitate Third Baptist just because they are successful, that may be a very wrong assumption. There is one area where I qualify this statement in Guideline #3.*

So, your mission may be staring you in the face. Yet you haven't acknowledged it. That may be because it isn't as high profile as Third Baptist's celebrity ministry. Or it may be because it doesn't

Life Event Number 2 - Noah

place your church in the light of glory that your flesh secretly craves. I think all of us would love to bear the cross of Reverend Will B. Dunn and minister to the fabulously rich and well-to-do (Doug Marlette, 1982-2007). But God may instead give you an inner-city ward that defines your purpose. God may direct you to a very narrow target population, such as college students at a nearby college or university.

By way of example, our church shifted its ministry emphasis with our change in leadership. Our previous pastor brought an evangelistic calling, which colored his entire ministry characterized by mission endeavors worldwide. One leg of our mission ministry supported ministers in their native countries; the second leg supported missionaries. Our mission program regularly brought in these pastors and missionaries to talk about their ministries. That face-to-face encounter created a real sense of partnership with "boots on the ground" in contrast to "pictures on a page." It instilled in us a realization that "this stuff is truly happening." My favorite was The Ghost. He was a pastor in Africa whom God delivered from more than one assassination attempt. Hence, he won the moniker "The Ghost."

On the home front, our pastor also had a tremendous anointing for healing broken relationships. The result was to restore and heal families who experience brokenness and wounded hearts in their own family of origin. He strove to bring folks back that had strayed far away from the Lord and conflictual individuals who have never experienced the power and grace of His salvation. His unique talents, gifts, and ministries inspired us in our efforts to achieve our preordained purpose under his leadership.

Under our current Sr Pastor, our focus is disciple-making, and the theme is Disciples Making Disciples. As an outgrowth of this, other ministries have sprung up spearheaded by laymen, most notably a ministry to widows that focuses on home maintenance and repairs. Another one is a restoration ministry focusing on addictions. While these latter ministries don't have disciple-making as their core objective, it is an affiliated byproduct. For example, the restoration ministry's goal is to end addictions, but what do you do with people who are in the process of overcoming addictions or after they have overcome their addiction? You disciple them. The central theme of the widow's ministry is to meet logistical household needs. I'm sure there is more disciple-making going on than anyone is aware of or tracking. That's the kind of thing that happens when we align our plans and our efforts with God's objective. So, purpose can be as broad as a ministry philosophy or as narrow as a specific ministry goal.

It's Your Choice - Is our purpose assured because we have been offered this opportunity to partner with God? Not if we don't accept the offer. But if our core motive is to obey God, how can it not be assured? Understand that we have a binary existence. What does that mean? By now, you may have surmised that I'm somewhat of a fatalist regarding our right or authority to select our spiritual destination or set our course in getting there. Here is the binary principle: we can choose to say <u>yes</u> or <u>no</u> to God, but we cannot decide its consequences. We cannot select the "whys" or "wherefores" once we say yes. It's not a question of God giving us the directive and us saying, "Thanks, we'll take it from here."

To say yes to God is to build on a spiritual foundation; to say no to God is to build on a fleshly foundation. There is no third choice. Procrastination is a "no." Also, we cannot decide that the third choice is to do it our way and call that building on a spiritual foundation – Romans 8:7. In support of my stance on this issue, here is another piece of insight from Romans, *not of works but of Him who calls* (Romans 9:11). While this is an oblique application, it says our spiritual path forward and resulting destination are established by God, not by our choice or ability. For scriptural support, see Ephesians 2:10: *For we are His workmanship, created in Christ Jesus for good works, which God prepared beforehand that we <u>should walk in them</u>.*

So purpose is not assured if we don't accept the offer to partner with God. Neither is our success guaranteed merely by acknowledging our mission objective. In other words, if we recognize our mission but then park it on the bookshelf, our purpose becomes moot and is not assured. It's similar to the scenario I painted where the young woman is called to child evangelism but does nothing about it for decades. We need to embrace our mission objective by stepping out in faith to fulfill it in partnership with God. In this fashion, we have a choice to activate it or not. It's not in our nature to align our plans with God's (as if we have any authority to make plans). It is in our disposition to make plans and expect God to align Himself with us. But because God doesn't talk to us verbally, there is always some level of uncertainty about whose plan it is. Is what we think is God's plan indeed God's plan?

<u>**Key Insight for Prayer:**</u> It should always be our prayer that our plans and God's plans would be in perfect agreement. Our churches will automatically receive blessings as a consequence.

It's Not Your Choice. - We need to distance ourselves from the perception that our responsibility is to establish our destination, set our course, and steer our ship. That's not to say we won't put in a good deal of work and enduring hardships on board. Lord knows

Israel fought their fair share of battles on the way to the promised land, but how many of those did they win because of Moses' superior leadership skills. And how many campaigns did they win because Israel functioned as God's weapon to win those battles. Don't forget the times Israel lost conflicts and why they lost them. They never lost a fight when they were in the center of God's will.

<u>Key Insights for Prayer</u>: Because of man's stubborn streak to pilot his ship, the "how" of our prayers should be that God

1. Will give the *church leadership* a spirit of discernment to recognize God's call and answer in the affirmative, and
2. Will give the *church membership* a spirit of discernment to recognize God's call and answer in the affirmative.

So, you see, it operates on two levels: leadership and membership.

In concluding this discussion, how do we become aware of our purpose? That will be Rule #2. I won't belabor the point; Rule #2 is straightforward.

Rule #2: see Rule #1

You must be desperate to honor God with Your life.

20/20 is Vital – We've been driving hard on the idea of Purpose, so before we wind up our discussion, let's break the grind by digressing to a related point. I want to tie up one other loose end necessary for completing our mission on assignment for God. I've dropped the term several times, but I avoided highlighting it because it would have distracted the discussion's focus. I want to draw attention to it here. Behind every resolute decision and action is *vision*. That is what enables us to visualize what God has for the church. When He casts a vision in our hearts and minds, goals and plans follow, and dreams become a reality. We must pursue it with diligence. It will materialize in God's appointed time. Our job is to have faith and confidence in Him to see it come to pass and become a reality. Without vision, God's work will never have the meaning and spiritual vim, vigor, and vitality the Father intends for us to have as the body of Christ. The scripture goes so far as to say that we will ultimately perish without it. To fully experience this concept's full impact, we need to view Proverbs 29:18 through the eyes of two versions of the Bible.

> *Where there is no vision, the people <u>perish</u>: but he that keepeth the law, happy is he. (KJV).*

> *Where there is no revelation, the people <u>cast off restraint</u>; But happy is he who keeps the law. (NKJV)*

Note the phrase "cast off restraint." That is what I call an epiphany. We will focus more on vision under our last Life Event on Joseph.

<u>**Key Insight for Prayer:**</u> Pray that your church will remain true to its vision and mission. Pray that your church also formulates a mission statement that reflects intent as well as objective. May they dream big things with a big God.

Guideline Wrap Up: What is Your Purpose?

Welcome to My Mind - Now, despite my calm assurances, you may have decided that we've gotten completely lost in our house of mirrors. And where we came out isn't exactly where we went in. Thank you for noticing. Or, in going through the woods, some may go so far as to say we got hopelessly lost and ended up way off

Life Event Number 2 - Noah

course. I would be more inclined to say we started off track and ended up on the right path. Why didn't I skip all the early discussions and just focus on the latter end? There is a twofold reason. Earlier I said, "I won't start with a textbook definition of purpose; rather, I will start where I believe most of us reside conceptually."

I really don't know where you were at the beginning of this discussion, but I know where I was in the not-too-distant past, and I further surmised that others like me are out there. I took you through a thought maze that started where my understanding started. In all honesty, I'm not sure I would have accepted the latter end if someone presented it to me at the beginning. I would have taken it as spiritually naïve at best and juvenile or impractical at worst.

I wanted you to experience how my understanding progressed. I am neither an articulate thinker nor an impromptu speaker. It is like I'm rambling through a thicket with poorly defined paths when I think things through. I go down dead ends, go on parallel trails, take forks that end up in rabbit trails, or deviate far from my intended destination. My spiritual side must battle with my fleshly side. But eventually, I end up back on track, and the net effect is that I now know I'm on the right path. There is no doubt in my mind as to whether any of the side trails or forks might be the correct path; I know they are not, and I know why they are not.

None of us can ever start from where we are not. So for the sake of those like me, I took us through this process together. There is only one master reason for a ministry initiative in the final analysis: to obey God. Would you have accepted that singular conclusion if I presented it first? Now you can have as many associated reasons as you want as long as they are compatible with and subordinate to the master reason to obey God. I'm not sure any other reasons have any value, but you can have as many as you want.

In approaching the end of our trek, I present you with a challenge. Should you question why your leadership, your church, your fellow church members, and you, in particular, are embarking on a ministry initiative? Absolutely! Understand, however, that is one of those situations in which discernment wins out over objectivity. In reprising the earlier discussion on polling the leadership and fellow members, you are not likely to know whether their answer is truth or spin. You will need to exercise discernment. Pay attention to that nagging discomfort in the back of your mind that something is not quite right. Granted, those who are participating out of obedience to God will gladly tell you so. Those who aren't won't say so; instead, they are likely to see it implied in their actions irrespective of their personal bias. That is, they interpret the availability of a ministry opportunity as an indirect invitation to obedience. While that may be true, why not say so in the first place? Why not promote that reason to number one?

Then there is the category of people who consider themselves free agents to pursue whatever ministry comes across their desk. They believe it's up to their discretion to pick and choose which ones to pursue. These might include leaders who follow the philosophy of "Thank you, God, we'll take it from here." – not an act of obedience but an act of taking advantage of an opportunity. Although this latter case represents a partnership, it's a wrong kind of collaboration because it suggests an alliance of equality and not an association of submission. These folks might consider obedience to God as so broadly defined that no ministry pursued can be construed as disobedient to God. In the final analysis, no one will confess to chasing a ministry initiative independent of obedience to God.

When there is no clearly defined motive or if the reason given is anything other than obedience to God, that should be a red flag. Any effort to confront the leadership is not likely to yield conclusive results and is more likely to be relationally destructive. By prayer and probably only by prayer will they redirect to embrace the right reason. If, in the final analysis, you feel confrontation is necessary, take a page from Esther's playbook when Mordecai admonished her to approach the King regarding the pending genocide of the Jews. Just let your spouse know in advance that you are inviting the pastor to dinner.

Key Insight for Prayer: Pray that your leadership will always embrace the right reason for pursuing a ministry initiative - just to obey God.

So, in retrospect, did I get off into the weeds a little? Yes, I did. Did I muddy the waters somewhat? You bet! Did I run the ball past the goalposts and into the parking lot? Probably. Taking you through this protracted thought exercise was, in part, to give you an all-encompassing understanding of purpose. It was also to demonstrate there is a likelihood that we are confused about what our core purpose is. It really can be like a house of mirrors, particularly if you don't know you are in one. However, my primary motive was to give you pause to think about your church ministry's core purpose and not be sidetracked by peripheral goals. That applies to ministries, new or old. Sometimes it's necessary to get lost in the weeds to appreciate the trail.

Membership Focus: *At this juncture, do you think your membership really understands your new ministry's core purpose or just think they do?*

Only "Thee Lord" Can Lead in Mutually Exclusive Directions - I close with a statement that many probably thought I should have opened. I'm guessing that 99.99% to 100% of all ministry initiatives start with this statement. *"We believe the Lord is leading us to (you fill in the blank)."* No legitimate church leader would dare propose a ministry initiative without prefacing it with that statement. But do they mean it? Or is it church rhetoric that just pops out of their mouth like other habitual phrases we use in everyday conversation? I didn't start with it because it is too subjective and too easily abused. I have heard the *"will of the Lord"* invoked to defend both sides of the issue.

Some in the leadership hierarchy will likely use that phrase as leverage to get their way. So how do you know the difference, and what could you do about it if you did? Is it possible that the leadership would knowingly pursue a ministry initiative out of God's will? They probably wouldn't, but they are very likely to base their decision on seeing a choice prospect or the opportunity for advancement. Again, neither is wrong if obedience to God is the actual motive and not an excuse, which has to do with the following guideline. We will revisit this aspect of both sides invoking the Lord's will when I relate the story of one church's experience in planting a second campus.

We've reached the end of our trek on purpose (pun intended), but there is more to Noah's life event.

Guideline #3: Begin with The Proper Foundation

Applicability

- **Target Population:** Church Leadership (Pastor, Elders, Deacons)

I Cor. 3:13: *each one's work will become clear; for the Day will declare it, because it will be revealed by fire; and the fire will test each one's work, of what sort it is.*

Topical Delineation and Elaboration

Parable of the Faithful Apprentice and the Unfaithful Apprentice

The Faithful Apprentice - Noah stayed close to the master architect and His blueprints. He knew the importance of building very wisely from the beginning. The Ark's foundation was crucial. Otherwise, it would have never withstood the torrents of rain and incredible floods that lasted 40 days and 40 nights. He began very astutely, and so should we. Noah began by erecting a secure and stable foundation. That applies both in a physical sense and a spiritual sense. Noah was wise in knowing that the spiritual foundation he had already laid for himself and his family needed to be built and maintained upon God. As alluded to earlier, this latter foundation was why God called him to erect the Ark's foundation.

Noah knew this, and his prayers must have mirrored this fact too.

Key Insight for Prayer: In the spirit of Noah, we should pray that every one of our beginnings has a secure foundation.

Membership Focus: *How does all this translate into your church life? Just this, rest in the confidence that Jesus Christ is the Master Builder, and it's His blueprint from which we are working (a loose application of Hebrews 11:10). How you build your church's foundation, fellow prayer warrior, will have serious future consequences for good or for bad.*

No construction company would ever consider starting a commercial construction project with drawings a licensed engineer had not sealed. No construction company would ever say, "we can't wait on the engineer; we need to start now." God's word teaches us that there are only two foundations that we can build upon regardless of how lofty our goals, plans, and ideals are. We will either lay our foundation on things of the spirit or things of the flesh.

Membership Focus: *While this is true, we don't decide in practice whether to lay our foundation on things of the spirit or things of the flesh. We choose either to establish it on things of the Spirit or not to found it on things of the Spirit. Specific indicators will enable you to know which of the two you choose. For example, there is undue concern over financial resources necessary to launch new works founded on the flesh. The church leadership and membership will limit their potential by what they can <u>afford</u>, and in doing so, reduce the power of God to that of man.*

The Unfaithful Apprentice - In reality, few if any churches will lay their foundation entirely on the flesh. But I would venture to say that there are even fewer who found it wholly on things of the spirit. Hence, it's a question of where in the spectrum between the two extremes one lies. When a church lays its foundation on things of the flesh, that is the business model I spoke of earlier. For a business, that is fine; for a church, it can be very damning. In the extreme position, this church arrives at the point of walking by "sight," of *having the form of godliness but denying its power* (2 Tim. 3:5).

Glorifying God is a necessary ingredient in your recipe for success. It is enormously fulfilling, and the blessing of fulfillment is stupendous. A sense of satisfaction is the precursor to joy and happiness, and who doesn't want to be joyous and happy? Did I just take a hard left without signaling? What does glorifying God have to do with working from His blueprint? As we detailed in the last guideline, we are in partnership with God, and He is the Sr. partner. He also decides who will receive his blueprints, a decision based on our disposition toward him. Would you pick someone to be your Jr. partner who speaks highly of you but for some reason, you get the distinct impression they don't mean it because...

Actions Speak Louder Than Words?

Side note: Do you know why clichés are clichés? It's because they are so valid. So, when I use a cliché, don't be so ready to dismiss it as rhetoric or trying to be cute.

Membership Focus: *Remember that it is not necessary to spiritualize every principle we talk about here. If you are starting a new church on undeveloped land, then builder beware. Utilizing high-quality building materials to build a durable, sturdy building and secure foundation will make a world of difference for your structure. Compromise will spell ongoing maintenance headaches, and everything will eventually cost more to maintain than your church has resources. Be a good steward of your God-given resources. Pay the price for excellence and build only with the best.*

As the old advertising slogan goes, "The quality goes in before the name goes on" (Zenith Electronics, 1927).

<u>Key Insight for Prayer:</u> One of your roles as a prayer warrior is to pray for the physical foundation upon which your church builds. Pray that the construction planners in your church will stand firm in their conviction not to compromise when pressured to do so.

Materials are Material: Countering Inexorable Decline

How do we avoid the calamity of a faulty spiritual foundation? What materials do we need to start gathering to guarantee our success?

Acclimation Mitigation – To some extent, we are all acclimated to the worldly system, so I can't counsel how to avoid it. I can, however, counsel how to reverse it. First, you need a daily "to-do" list, one that is very short. Rank scripture memorization and meditation at the top of your list. That's it, that's your list. Here is why that is important. We become immersed in the secular environment, much like you submerge a brand-new tropical fish (still in the plastic baggy) in your aquarium. You do this to allow the water temperature in the baggy to equalize with the aquarium's temperature. By analogy, the secular world represents the aquarium in which we become immersed. That secular water bath causes us to become increasingly desensitized to moral values. As a result, we move toward the amoral disposition of the worldly system, hence the statement "first we abhor, then we tolerate, and then we embrace." Scripture memorization and meditation are deliberate acts that compensate or reverse the relentless drift toward worldly philosophy.

Investment Strategy - Second, serving and investing in the lives of others is a must. How does this latter component relate to good foundations? Whether you realize it or not, you are more a part of the foundation than any logistical preparation you are making to ensure your ministry's success. If the people who make up the church are not firmly rooted in Christ and the Word, how will they ever minister to your church's target group? Remember, if you do not invest yourself, you have no vested interest.

Key Insight for Prayer: Pray for the spiritual foundation that your church builds upon in its formative growth process. Pray that ministry participants would understand they are that foundation. The strength of that foundation is a function of scripture meditation and how they invest themselves in others.

Membership Focus: *If your church was founded long ago, ask for a word of discernment on how all this went - primarily God-directed or man-directed. If the latter appears to be the case, pray for reconfiguration of your church's spiritual foundation. Pray for the conviction to seek out guidance and the courage to step out of your comfort zone and risk operating under a different paradigm that is God-directed. Note; however, you can't turn a ship (or a church) on a dime.*

What is Reality?

Most Means Most - In qualifying the above Membership Focus, I make the following blanket statement. M<u>ost</u> new church foundings are God-directed. Not only does my personal experience bear witness to this, but I believe this is so for several reasons. The chief is that God has foreknowledge of where He wants His new churches to go. So, God is probably at the finish line by the time elders of a flesh-driven church react. God has already lined up his spirit-driven church to start building, while leaders of the flesh-driven church are still arguing about whether to pounce on the opportunity.

A second reason involves our favorite battleground issue – finances. Most churches are too preoccupied with financial constraints to take on another financial burden without God's directive.

A third reason is one I can speak of from personal experience, and that is spiritual cognition. This one may be more relevant than the reason just cited. Take it from one who has drifted in and out of spiritual awareness. I can tell you from experience, anyone operating from a fleshly mindset doesn't have the spiritual cognition to dream dreams about new churches. Anyone in the fog of a fleshly mentality is incapable of comprehending spiritually transcendent dreams and ambitions.

Rare but True - Please don't take my blanket statement as a nullification of Guideline #1; begin with God. In our current social climate, Guideline #1 becomes all the more significant. In reconciling this apparent contradiction, you will recall my statement that *most* church foundings are God-directed. There are two scenarios I can imagine in which a church founding is potentially man-directed. The first is a church split. Don't automatically assume that the body of believers breaking off from the Mother Church is wrong. There are actual cases in which the Mother Church was too tolerant. However, in cases where the Mother Church is in the right, the breakaway church has no option but to be man-directed.

The other scenario is if the Mother Church has deep pockets or the founding organization is a denomination and not a local church body. That doesn't mean large churches or denominations are flesh-driven. It does mean that any organization with wealth can plant a church if they want to – with or without God's directive. You can be a spirit-driven church and still make an occasional flesh-driven decision. If King David did it, so can we. That was neither a compliment nor permission. In the integrity of their heart, a large church or a denomination can assume that God wants them to build a new campus in a new neighborhood without actually consulting Him.

Membership Focus: *More than likely, your church's founding was God-directed, and perhaps sometime later, invasive weeds crept in and dominated the landscape, causing a shift toward materialism. What if you are a member of such a church whose foundation has slowly shifted from a spiritual foundation to one of materialism or one contaminated by subtle forms of false doctrine? In either case, the church can prosper in a measure. However, I would deem it unlikely that they would have little more than a cultural influence on the community. That is not a task that you can physically tackle by presenting your case to the leadership. We already discussed this above in Adam and Eve. My experience is that a course correction occurs only through a turnover in leadership. Hence, don't rule this out as a viable goal toward which you should pray.*

Key Insight for Prayer: Pray that God will lift the fog or remove the blinders materialism and false doctrine place over the leadership's eyes.

Guideline Wrap Up: Foundational Indicators

Weathering Time - How do you recognize when a church builds its ministry upon a godly foundation versus a fleshly foundation?

1. God always builds a godly foundation on the slab of trials and testing.

   Sorry to disappoint you, but it's true. False teachers who teach you about foundations will tell you that hardship is unnecessary when laying a foundation. That is very contrary to Scripture. In Jesus' life, we know that the testing and temptations he underwent routinely helped prepare him for what he would suffer upon the cruel cross.

   ...though he was a Son, yet He learned obedience by the things which he suffered. And having been perfected, He became the author of eternal salvation to all who obey Him (Hebrews 5:8 & 9)

   and

   ...may the God of all grace, who called us to His eternal glory by Christ Jesus, after you have suffered a while, perfect, establish, strengthen, and settle you. (1st Peter 5:10)

   He saw these trials through grace-tinted glasses, and we should view them that way too. That doesn't mean He was naïve about the harsh realities of life. It means He understood what was at stake in the mission He was tasked with and couldn't let the discomfort of trials dissuade Him from His goal of salvation by grace.

2. You can never build a good and reliable foundation immediately or hastily.

Life Event Number 2 - Noah

It takes time and patience and requires great skill, workmanship, and craftsmanship; it merely will not happen overnight. So, give yourself time to grow! That is why you must work with the group of complementary spiritual gifts that God has entrusted to your membership and not the "qualified candidates" with briefcases 50 miles from home. A legitimate question might be: should you put your new ministry on hold until you've grown more mature? No. This rule has both short-term and long-term applications. You can't reap the long-term benefits if you don't apply this rule in the immediate. God will bless the short-term efforts if your membership is not where it should be maturity-wise.

Does your church need to change cornerstones? The Bible tells us that Jesus is the chief cornerstone. A cornerstone is the starting point of a building's foundation.

The Present Will Become the Past - Consider this point before we move on to Guideline #4. During the years Noah spent building the Ark, how much time do you think he spent musing on the aftermath? He endured the physical stress of cutting the timber, transporting it to the job site, shaping and fitting it, assembling and waterproofing it. Add to this the emotional turmoil of putting up with his neighbors. Everything probably focused on the moment when, as some would say, "it's showtime." The Flood came, and the Flood went. At that point, all the hardships were in the past and probably forgotten.

Membership Focus: *So too will all the hardships from which you now suffer be forgotten one day. The only way they can come back to haunt you is if you compromised. Any form of compromise can hinder your progress or derail you from reaching your destination. But once you get to your destination, all those trials and hardships* *can't hurt you anymore. A note from Mark: when I pass the healthcare facilities where Rebecca spent her last days, I remind myself that she will never have to suffer through that again.*

As we were saying, the Flood came, and the Flood went, and then what? That brings us to our last Guideline for Noah.

Guideline #4: Begin with Something New

Applicability

- **Target Population:** Church Body at Large

Isaiah 43:19: *Behold I will do a new thing, now it shall spring forth; shall you not know it? I will even make a road in the wilderness and rivers in the desert.*

Topical Delineation and Elaboration

Can New Be Negotiated?

Adam and Eve is understandably the prototype of something new. New, however, can also apply to a situation in which we come out of something old. When God hit the restart button, Noah was his instrument of something new: a new civilization.

Membership Focus: *Do you ever wonder when it's God's time to launch out into something new? It doesn't have to be a new mission church or establishing a second campus.*

Many churches frequently find themselves face to face with the need to change or close the doors. Unfortunately, this is where we get into the unpleasant task of trying to put new wine into old wineskins. The traditionalists in any church will resist any paradigm shift tooth and nail because their methods worked quite well in their generation. They see them as sacred. One of the churches I was a member of went through this phase. The fear expressed by the traditionalists was that venerable biblical doctrines would get watered down to make them palatable to current societal norms in the name of "reaching the lost." We referred to the traditionalists as the old guard.

The new guard's fear was we would not be attractive to Gen-X if we didn't change. They rightly feared we would die on the vine, having no relevance to a generation of essentially "unchurched" people. They didn't call them "lost" anymore; that was judgmental, religious jargon, and carried the stigma of an outdated idea that being "lost" is a valid truth.

In this battle of the generations, we found ourselves wrestling with the polar opposite concepts of *negotiables* and *non-negotiables*. Fortunately, we had godly leaders that saw biblical doctrines as sacred. Generally, the non-negotiables were along doctrinal lines, and the negotiables were along methodological lines. As you may guess, church choirs and hymnals were among the fatalities of that battle. Praise bands and praise song lyrics on the overhead screen supplanted them. To this day, I still run across people looking for traditional churches that still sing from hymnals and have choirs. What floors me is how current-generation church leaders with praise bands will continually laud church choirs as a significant worship component. Still, for some reason, they never get past lauding.

Membership Focus: *Concerning your church, what kind(s) of change does God want to bring about the most? What things does He want to remain the same? What thoughts, ideas, and* *approaches have worked best in the past? Do they still work now? Which ones have a proven track record? Which ones have brought about a less than desirable result? What indications for change do you need to contemplate? How can you pray for their materialization? When should you pray for their inception? In what manner do you pray for the rebirth of approaches that have served you well? Or do you need to pray for a revelation of new strategies?*

Micromanaging vs. Macromanaging

I know the above membership focus appears to fly in the face of my previous discussion on letting God micromanage our ministries. As expressed here, it sounds like we are the decision-makers in determining what works and what is best. I still stand by my original premise of walking in lockstep with God, but how much wiggle room is there within the context of that stance? If we think about what has worked before and what hasn't, does that mean we rely on our own experience, not the Holy Spirit's guidance? So, the question I pose is this. Does God's perfect instructional plan include letting us chart our course, make mistakes, and stumble along? Or is it an indication that we are not paying attention to God's directions? My opinion is that God's plan is as perfect as we will let it be. It all goes back to the following tandem principle:

1. We have the right to choose yes or no, and
2. God can do it without us, but He won't do it without us.

Does God hold these departures against us? Probably not, if "in the integrity of our heart," we honestly thought we were following His plan. As long as we set a precedent of returning to His guidance, I think most of our mistakes come under the category of the "learning curve." In this, we suffer the consequences of our errors, but He calls us to get up and move past them. Only when we get bull-headed in walking in our wisdom does God send leanness to our church. In the extreme, He takes our candle stand away.

Membership Focus: *So, when you consider what has and hasn't worked before, that's a good indicator that the consequences of your mistakes have had their intended effect.*

How does God's will fit into this dynamic interplay of the consequences of disobedience vs. the benefits of obedience? It's a two-sided coin. Heads, we wouldn't have made the mistakes if we were in perfect lockstep with God (not a likely scenario). Tails, allowing us to fail and suffer the consequences, is God's way of teaching us how not to do it. Failures with attendant costs become ingrained in our being. They help us develop maturity in navigating life according to God's principles. That way, He doesn't have to micromanage us every step of the way. So yes, there is some wiggle room.

Think of it as an intoxicated person walking down the hallway; they repeatedly go back and forth banging into the walls. Eventually, however, they get to the end of the hallway – very inefficient, but it works if you want that pathway. Now don't confuse the consequences of these mistakes with trials and tribulations incurred by invading the secular world's domain. Both are character-building, and both are beneficial from an experiential perspective. However, the aftermaths of our mistakes are on us and us alone. While God uses the consequences of our errors, I'm sure they are not His first choice in maturing us.

No Final Conflict

In considering negotiables and non-negotiables, no conflict should exist between biblical ministry models and historical methodologies. In other words, historical models and present-day methods should not violate biblical doctrines, even if they conflict with one another. These are the negotiables, and these are the ones that change from generation to generation.

That said, there are non-negotiables incorporated into the negotiables. Let me relate an example to help differentiate between non-negotiable principles and negotiable methodologies. Upon my father's passing, we went through his library of books and other literature he accumulated over the years and deciding what was salvageable and what wasn't. I came across several "how-to" books on developing church programs that ministered to the various age groups within the church population of the mid-20th century (post World War II generation).

Before I relate what I found, fast forward to the early 1990s when a new paradigm arose called "Home Fellowship Groups." Ralph Neighbour Jr. was the first minister I knew of who pioneered this new church model in our country and laid it out in his book "Where Do We Go From Here" (1990). Numerous other ministers quickly followed Dr. Neighbour's model and established their reputation through this new approach. The current term for "Home Fellowship Groups" is "Small Groups." Their primary intent is to minister to people at the personal level, in contrast to megachurches, mega Sunday school classes, and mass worship that foster an easy path to getting "lost in a crowd." Small groups have met with great success in many local church congregations. Small groups have replaced or complemented their outreach program and the current paradigm of ministering to their congregants.

Membership Focus: *So, if you are in a traditional church, it could be time for your church to launch some and see if they are right for you.*

Now here is what I found in those "how-to" books. They taught precisely the same principle for ministering to individuals as prescribed by the multitude of ministers who jumped on the "small group" bandwagon. These same principles continue to be taught today, except for one difference. The present-day church approaches it through small groups that meet in homes and the church throughout the week. The mid-20th century church did the same thing on Sunday mornings and Wednesday nights within the church walls. They had it down to a fine art of limiting Sunday school classes to about 8 or 10 individuals, thereby giving individual attention to each person. That methodology worked in the mid-20th century when the church was an integral part of our culture. At that time, a much larger segment of the population attended church. Of course, small groups were all they had in rural America; they didn't have a choice. By extension, however, most metropolitan areas comprised neighborhoods that weren't very different from rural towns because many urbanites were rural folks who came to town.

Course Correction

Were they ahead of their time in the mid-20th century? I wouldn't say so; I would say we just lost our way over time – remember the concept of creep or drift we discussed in Adam & Eve. Small groups within the confines of the church worked in post-WWII America because they operated in the dominant cultural context of the church. They declined in their effectiveness in the mid 20th century (the late 1960s to early 1970s) because of urban expansion. Church growth tracking with that expansion was either unable or unwilling to give individual attention to their members. That resulted in a growing disenchantment with organized denominations. By then, small groups were a forgotten part of the past. Rediscovered at the end of the 20th century, "small groups" were perceived as a new concept.

The reason for their effective resurgence was because small groups went to the populace. The populace was not required to go to church. Interestingly, that was the New Testament model portrayed in the book of Acts. But generally, "the populace" came to church once they joined a small group and found it non-threatening. The basic concept is that "unchurched" folks will go to their neighbor's home, who they know. But they won't go to a church that they don't know and makes them feel very much out of their element. So, it appears that the principle of small groups is non-negotiable. The scriptures don't explicitly promote small groups. But, they seem to be a common-sense approach to discipling, exemplified historically by teachers surrounding themselves with a small band of students or disciples. The one case we are familiar with is Jesus and His small group of 12 disciples. To my knowledge, you won't find anywhere in new testament scripture that disciple-making is best done in small groups. Nor does scripture speak of the size of those groups. The negotiable aspect is how we administer the small groups – in the church or the homes.

What does this have to do with praying for your church? We can take away two prayer pointers from this discussion:

Key Insight for Prayer:

1. Pray that we can differentiate between non-negotiable principles of ministry and negotiable "how-to" methodologies in administering those principles, and

2. Pray that we don't throw the baby out with the bathwater by forsaking timeless ministry principles on the basis that older methodologies don't appeal to the current generation.

As it turns out, ministry models are not standalone. They should be considered only in context with current societal norms and **one** master non-negotiable. The one non-negotiable is that we have received a spiritual mandate from God to commence with something new. Now let's close the loop on our discussion. We started by asking a series of questions centered on the one question of when it's God's timing to launch into something new. I surmise it falls in line with changes in societal norms that we briefly touched on above. Don't jump to the conclusion that God's standards change with society. He doesn't change, but His methodologies may. Anytime I advocate changes to address societal norms, I'm not talking about shifting our standards to accommodate society. I'm talking about changing our ministry approach to speak to secular society's needs. If we can't speak their language, we can't win them to Christ.

Guideline Wrap Up: Gathering our Threads on Paradigm Shifts

Here are some factors and indicators that drive the need for paradigm shifts:

1. There are changes in the current population profiles or demographics.

Life Event Number 2 - Noah

2. New times and eras are rising, characterized by shifting social customs that dictate the need for change (i.e., a new pharaoh has arisen that doesn't know Joseph).

3. The old generation is diminishing in size, and the younger future generation is up and coming.

   a. They need to be trained and taught to step into new roles and places of leadership – leadership principles don't change.

   b. They have their way of doing things. Keeping our kids grounded firmly in the Word will help ensure that they don't forsake the underlying non-negotiable principles in the process of changing methodology.

   c. Your current or former endeavors do not appear to be doing as well. They have outgrown their effectiveness and continue to wane in their usefulness.

   For example, tent revivals with fire and brimstone sermons just don't seem to draw Gen Xrs or the Millennials like they did in my Parents' Day. They didn't even bring in Baby Boomers. Growing up, we used to have week-long revivals. They weren't fire and brimstone, but they were mountain top experiences that gave us a spiritual jump start. They dwindled to 3-day revivals, and now I rarely hear about them anymore.

4. Neighboring church bodies similar in size to yours are instituting new methods, ministries, and programs. They have proven to be very successful. Careful, we've discussed this above. Some ministries relate to your church's unique calling. Others, such as small groups, are universal because they cater to a new societal norm.

5. Old spiritual leaders and mentors have rolled off the active role for various reasons.

6. Past mistakes, old hurts, and wounds from the past have crippled the membership. Healing needs to take place. Roots of bitterness and anger need to be destroyed or addressed. That doesn't necessarily fit with the above discussion. However, it still applies to the concept of God wanting to launch something new.

7. Spiritual stagnation has hamstrung your church's ministry and robbed it of peace and joy. A new touch from the Lord is necessary to see your church's work grow and realize its full potential. Revival may be in the air. A health check would be a wise and sensible move. A thorough historical appraisal or statistical analysis and financial feasibility study may be advisable. A fresh beginning may be in order.

8. Your existing church ministries have become problematic. You seem to have more problems than solutions. You are experiencing a ministerial crisis, or you feel that one is very eminent or just around the corner. While this is vague to the average reader, this item should jump out at anyone whose church is suffering from problematic ministries.

Items 1 through 5 relate to being current with societal norms. Have you started to feel the impact of the times in which you now live? Are the signs of the times popping up right before your eyes? Are you keeping pace with them, or are you lagging? A new generation of folks is coming of age, and they respond only to their generation's ways of doing things. The old is passé. Items 6 through 8 relate to fleshly tendencies that get a toehold in any given church.

Life Event Number 2 - Noah

Should the Lord grant me a long life, we will postpone discussing that topic until Ezra and Nehemiah.

Following is the summary list of prayer pointers covered under our treatment of Noah, which you can skip and return to later if you want a quick reference.

Summary List of Prayer Pointers from Noah

- Pray that your plans and God's plans would always be in perfect agreement.
- Pray that God will give the church leadership a spirit of discernment to recognize God's call and answer in the affirmative.
- Pray that God will give the church membership a spirit of discernment to recognize God's call and answer in the affirmative.
- Pray that your church will remain true to its vision and mission.
- Pray that your church formulates a mission statement that reflects intent as well as objective.
- Pray that your leadership will always embrace the right reason for pursuing a ministry initiative, just to obey God.
- Pray that every one of your beginnings starts with a secure foundation.
- Pray for the physical foundation upon which your church builds. Pray that the construction planners in your church will stand firm in their conviction not to compromise when pressured to do so.
- Pray for the spiritual foundation that your church builds upon in its formative growth process. Pray that ministry participants would understand they are that foundation. The strength of that foundation is a function of scripture meditation and how they invest themselves in others.

Life Event Number 2 - Noah

- ➢ Pray that God will lift the fog or remove the blinders materialism and false doctrine place over the leadership's eyes.

- ➢ Pray that your church can differentiate between non-negotiable principles of ministry and negotiable "how-to" methodologies in administering those principles.

- ➢ Pray that your church doesn't throw the baby out with the bathwater by forsaking timeless ministry principles on the basis that the older methodologies don't appeal to the current generation.

Life Event Number 2 - Noah

Life Event Number 3 - Abraham

Let's Take a Journey. Our third personality and life event involve another well-known biblical character, Abraham. His life can teach us much concerning prayer when we look at his journey because the most significant points center on a literal journey. God instructed Abram to leave the land of his father and journey to a foreign land. He had to take God at His word with little or no supporting evidence – at least none of which we know. What he does know is that God promised to make him the father of many nations, and He promised to be with him all the way – echoes of Purpose.

What an incredible promise! If God told me that, I would have looked behind me to see if He spoke to someone else. However, realistically, Abram must have wondered how this could take place. God's promises to him were unambiguous but had no basis in the reality Abram and Sarai knew. They had no male heirs, and there were none on the horizon. To make matters worse, they had no children at all.

In stepping out in obedience to God, they necessarily had to leave behind home and community. Indeed, they had to leave their entire support structure behind. They trusted God one day at a time. Their journey was so incredibly long, but they eked it out little by little, day by day – just he and Sarai. Don't count Lot and his wife or the herdsmen they took with them. These undoubtedly served to meet Abram's social needs. Still, none of these were required to fulfill God's promise to Abram and Sarai.

Note, I will refer to them as Abraham and Sarah when speaking in a general context. When speaking in the specific context of their journey (physically and spiritually), I will reference them as Abram and Sarai until about a year before Isaac comes along. That was when God visited them and not only informed them of Isaac's debut but changed their names to Abraham and Sarah.

Guideline #5: Begin with Obedience - Do Not Despise Small Beginnings.

Applicability

- **Target Populations:** This has multilevel applicability
    1. Your church body as an entity
    2. Any ministry spawned by your church body, and
    3. The rank and file church member

Zechariah 4:10: *For who has despised the day of small things?*

I include the rank and file church member as a target group because, like each church member, Abraham's story elicits an image of one man's journey. It portrays a picture of one who was alone with God in the wilderness. Even though he had his entourage of herdsmen, servants, and extended family, it was *his* calling and *his* journey, not anyone else's.

Topical Delineation and Elaboration

Abram did, in reality, start pretty small, so most of us should be able to relate to him. The story of how God strengthened Abram's faith as He took him from no status to international recognition should encourage us as we vicariously share his experience. What does the insignificance of his beginnings tell us about being a follower of God? How does it fit into the grand scheme of things for God's people?

Membership Focus: *God may not carry you and me to such magnificent heights. Nevertheless, He will always take us to glorious heights beyond our expectations if we follow His will and His plan for our daily lives. We are custom-made for that plan and vice versa. Sometimes though, we kind of feel stuck in the insignificance and the routine of it all. That's where Abraham can serve as such a marvelous example to all believers.*

Abraham's story provides us with one overarching guideline: Obedience. We kind of hammered on that idea in our discussion of Noah. But within this guideline, we expand obedience to encompass two components that go hand in hand and cannot be separated: *Small Beginnings* and *Faith*. You will see what I mean when I try to cover one without mentioning the other.

Membership Focus: *As you walk alone with God, you will expand your understanding of spiritual principles and how they intertwine. You will come to realize that one principle does not stand without the others. So too are the three components, obedience, faith, and small beginnings, as exemplified by Abraham.*

Broad Brush Strokes

We Weren't Born Yesterday - In the introduction to Genesis, I mentioned that beginnings are fundamental in the eyes of God. Case in point, name one thing born of God you have personally witnessed that materialized fully developed. We mature from babies to adults, and plants grow from seeds to trees. As God's handiwork, created in His image, we render our world according to the same pattern. Businesses develop from home offices to high-rises. Cities expand from communities to metropolitan areas. Countries grow from small independent villages to multistate nations, and churches grow from storefront mission plants to multi-campus behemoths. We see this growth phenomenon echoed throughout scripture. Specifically, Zechariah 4:10 admonishes us not to despise small beginnings. Ephesians 4:12-13 speaks of *edifying* (building up from small to great) *the body of Christ until we all come to the measure of the stature of the fullness of Christ* (from zero to Christ) (parenthetical comments added).

When Abram was nothing more than a tag-along behind his father, Terah, God promised to make him the father of many nations. That's an enormously incredible promise by anybody's standards. What makes it even more fascinating is that Abram was 75 years old when God made that promise. Practically speaking, that was impossible because, until this time, Abram's wife was completely infertile. Juxtapose the contrasting imagery of his insignificant status while in Haran against the global standing God promised him. Is it not noteworthy that Abram kept right on trusting the Lord?

Non-collateral Baggage - In the hopelessness of his posterity, Abram believed God against all odds. And that belief was counted unto him as righteousness (Gen. 15:6). Again I want to emphasize that Abram's status was not determined by who was part of his traveling company. I say this because we sometimes define high-profile people by their popularity and not how they won that status. The obvious application here is that your successes and failures belong to you, not the social circle you run in. Your social circle may fulfill your social needs, but it isn't responsible for ushering you into prominence. As indicated, Abram's entourage included Lot's family and Abram's share of sheepherders when he split off from brothers Nahor and Haran. Note: there are two Harans in the Genesis account: the town and Abram's brother.

When they parted company at Haran, the scripture is silent on whether Eliezer or Hagar was with them. They may have picked up Eliezer in Damascus on their way from Haran to Canaan. Scholars generally believe they picked up Hagar during their short sojourn in Egypt after reaching Canaan. So, details on Abram and Sarai's progeny that are common knowledge to us were unknown to them. That is, Eliezer, Abram's supposed heir, and Hagar, Sarai's surrogate, do not appear to have been in the picture when they left Haran. Hence, the options available to Abram and Sarai were slim to none when they parted company from their extended family.

Without a male heir and these other so-called viable options, starting with small beginnings is an understatement. They began with no realistic prospect of a future. All the other people in Abram's company were nonessentials to bringing about his progeny. But God was faithful to keep His promise, and He eventually gave Abram his son, Isaac. We will talk more about that in another guideline.

By our standards, I think Abram was middle to upper-middle-class when in Haran with Terah. I don't think starting small meant he was dirt poor. Whatever his financial status, Abram would have never learned what it meant to trust God if he was already wealthy, famous, and successful. If so, I believe it would have been next to impossible to respond to the command of a God Abram did not know. Recall the lesson of the rich young ruler in Luke 18. As touched on in Adam and Eve, the risk of loss becomes too high when your wealth comes to own you. Abram's heavenly father orchestrated it this way, and He taught Abram beautiful things amid his small, inconsequential beginnings. Abram did not resist His methods or His means. He did not look down on his early development, nor did he refuse to start at the beginning.

Parallel Pilgrimage - It's not hard to see how small beginnings in Abraham's life translate into a church or ministry's pilgrimage from inception to maturity. It's not difficult to see how they translate into the journey of individual members. Every living entity with a spiritual component experiences this pattern of growth. Individual Christians, churches, and ministries grow progressively and not by leaps and bounds.

Membership Focus: *There is no such thing as instant maturity. These tiny, small, and minute facets of your beginning are crucial to your future success and development. Hence, you must view these small beginnings as <u>never insignificant</u>. Why? What benefits and causalities can we find wrapped up in them? Just this:*

Our beginnings were not formed and fashioned out of nothing.

They were created and shaped by a particular mindset.

Becoming familiar with that mindset and the signposts along the way will help us focus our prayers so we can pray even more intensely.

The importance of small beginnings is conveyed succinctly in the following quote. *"Early sparks of faith will serve as our example of how you can increase your faith for things on down the road"* (anonymous - see footnote*). By way of an illustrative example:

> *He chose David also his servant and took him from the sheepfolds: From following the ewes great with young he brought him to feed Jacob his people, and Israel his inheritance. So, he fed them according to the integrity of his heart; and guided them by the skillfulness of his hands. Psalm 78:70-72 (KJV)*

An application of the anonymous quote is that no one needs to dread discipleship for fear that God will send them to Africa immediately. That was the fear when I was young; not sure what the current generation's fear is.

*Note from Mark: I'm sure Rebecca knew who quoted this, but I couldn't find the source.

Membership Focus: *Discipleship is a slow process. God is not going to call you to do anything you have not been prepared for, irrespective of whether you think you are ready or not. It applies to those who believe they are ready and those who don't.*

Let's draw out some prayer pointers here.

Key Insights for Prayer:

1. Pray that the saints in your church body would embrace this growth model from infancy to maturity as being ordained by God irrespective of their maturity level.
2. Pray that understanding the growth process would encourage and not discourage someone's decision to submit

to discipleship, start a new ministry, or even launch a new church.

3. Intercede for your church's leadership and all its ministry participants to not become overly ambitious and attempt to run faster than God wants you to run. Your church leadership's near-term goals should start at the pilot program level and build from there. Let me point out that limiting our ambition is purely for our benefit and in no way presumes any limitations on God. He can go as fast as He wants, but what is the point of inviting us along if we can't keep up? Think of yourself as a baby transitioning to toddlerhood and God as the adult helping you navigate this new walking skill. The converse is also true. Limitations of the target group may be the critical factor in how aggressively we move. In that case, God may want us to progress gradually.

4. Pray that immature saints in your church body would not avoid discipleship out of fear that they will have to forfeit their comfort zone.

5. Pray that all who have chosen to start a new ministry or submit to discipleship understand that testings and dry periods are part of the growth process. These, too, are ordained of God to produce character.

We will revisit this last prayer pointer later in this chapter.

Hierarchal Growth – Now, I want to discuss an aspect of growth only implied in Abraham's story. I believe it has a strong bearing on your level of commitment to follow God's path for you. I'm talking about individual experience versus collective experience. God did not tell Abram's social circle that He would make them a great nation. He revealed it to Abram. His company collectively experienced everything that happened as a result of Abram's calling. But, Abram was the target of God's calling, not his company. This same concept applies to each individual in your church body. Next, it applies to every ministry in your church and the church body itself at the intermediate and top levels, respectively.

Let's look at the individual level first. You are in community with others of like mind, and there is a camaraderie among those who surround you. Yet, your walk with God is yours and yours alone. Only you experience your successes and accomplishments, and only you experience your trials and failures. Sure, others can empathize with you or may even walk the same path in parallel with you. These fellow travelers can share in your hardships and disappointments, and yes, they can share in the exhilaration of your victories. Still, the way you are affected is different than the impact on your fellows. When it is time to go home, they do not carry your experiences with them; they take their own experiences home. Having a mountain top experience on a retreat is a good example. Upon returning home, others may rejoice with you in a measure. But they don't express the enthusiasm you do because they didn't go through the experience as you did.

Membership Focus: *How corporate experiences affect you is different from how they impact your fellow travelers. It changes you. These changes can sometimes bring you to a fork in the road where a choice confronts you. Are you prepared to choose a separate path?*

Now let's look at the ministry level, which includes specific target groups (children, widows, homebound, homeless, etc.). Contrast the ministries of which you are a part and those of which you are not. When your particular ministry group celebrates victories, do others exhibit the same sense of excitement? At the same time, when other ministry groups celebrate achievements, do you share the same level of excitement?

Finally, let's look briefly at the corporate level. I have a real-life story that illustrates how growth experiences can affect the direction a church body takes as a whole. It is the account of a church that founded its first satellite campus and joined the ranks of multicampus churches. The original intent, of course, was the new campus would be an extension of the Mother Church, and that worked out reasonably well for a while.

Over time, however, the new campus established itself in unique ways that differentiated it from the Mother Church. Contrary to expectations, the satellite campus took a different trajectory that eventually moved it into a different orbit. Instead of retaining it as a satellite campus, the Mother Church released it to be an independent church with a name of its own and a vision of its own. Because it all played out as a natural consequence of their community environment, they celebrated it as a gain, not a loss. More to come on this later.

Not All of Us Can Be Charter Members

Taking Ownership – Let me deviate from the main focus and address a particular case that doesn't fit this pattern exactly. For some of us, it may be more relevant than the discussion at hand. The concept of growth requires that most members join a church body after its inception and, in some cases, long after its inception. Can this fit into small beginnings for those who come along later? Or is that water under the bridge we can't claim? That is, you can't recover or reclaim what you never had. What bearing, if any, do the initial stages of a church's origins, growth, and spiritual development have on latecomers? The obvious answer is that non-charter members benefit from the efforts of others who planted and watered before. In one church where I was a member, they would regularly review their history to give new members a sense of ownership in that experience. The intent was to provide new members the impression that they were welcomed into the family as though they were always part of the family.

Membership Focus: *Likely, you were not there at the planting of your church. That missing history does not have to be a foreign component in your identity as one of its members. Take advantage of your church's origins by reviewing its history and taking post facto ownership of its beginnings. The net effect is that you have expanded your experiential reach from your church's beginning stages into its future phases. Isn't that worth taking ownership of your church's beginnings? The result is you will see that the fruits of your prayers are more beautiful, more productive, and significantly more personal. That is because you are praying for something in which you have become deeply invested.*

So, when a church publicly reviews its history, the benefit is to instill an appreciation of small beginnings. It expands our faith and enlarges our patience because progress according to God's standards is usually measured over a series of generations, not a series of winters. Moreover, taking ownership of our church's small beginnings can inspire and motivate us to become even more invested by giving more generously to the cause of Christ. In doing so, we realize that if we (collectively) don't pick up the baton and run with it, not only will our dreams fail to come true, but we will bring to naught the work of our predecessors.

Life Event Number 3 - Abraham

Key Insight for Prayer: Ask for a sense of ownership over your church's beginnings, current status, and future destiny.

You Can Get There from Here – What more substance can you add to your prayers? Let's continue with the scenario in which you joined a well-established church. That scenario probably applies to most church members. I want to zero in on you, the prayer warrior, here. Aside from the passive act of taking ownership of your church's beginning, you may wonder how you ever start at the beginning from a practical perspective. It's similar to the saying, "you can't get there from here."

Your origins will take on two levels. At the first level, your entry point into that congregation is your beginning. You may have the advantage of being a mature adult, but you are, otherwise, a virtual unknown. You are starting as a small potato in a congregation of strangers. Don't feel bad; if it's a large church, most are strangers to one another. An alternative scenario to this beginning is that you grew up in your church and are at that age where you want to test your wings. You have the advantage of being a known quantity, but you have no tested credibility. In either case, over time, you rise through the ranks of "whose who," just like Abram did. Not that you are striving for a position in "whose who." But if you expect to help chart the course on praying for your church, you need to be a recognized and trusted player. But should you have to strive for that? No. It should just happen as a natural consequence of your dedicated service.

Membership Focus: *I reiterate, becoming a trusted player should happen naturally for you. Nonetheless, it doesn't always happen that way because of factors discussed in Adam and Eve. If you find yourself in that position, your best recourse may be to put* *it in God's hands and let Him run interference for you. Unless you believe it to be an honest misunderstanding, confrontation probably will not make you a trusted player and may cause more harm than good.*

You Are Being Paged – This is where the second level of *small beginnings* occurs. As you become a trusted player on the prayer team, you will have more sway over the prayer team's direction. At this stage, your *new beginning* could potentially involve nothing more than a course correction as opposed to scrapping the whole program and starting over. Here is where it gets tricky; you are serving with those who joined the prayer team long before you did. Some of those were part of the group before you were born. I'm talking about those little old ladies who were there "before the woods was burned" and, to all appearances, seem to be immortal.

Possibly, the prayer group into which you have integrated has been in status quo mode for years. The original leader set up a system that was innovative at the time. All subsequent leaders maintained that same system out of respect for the originator. Alternatively, they saw the status quo as quite adequate or saw the established system as sacred and therefore untouchable. In other words, all the leaders since the original leader may have been managers, not visionaries. Now there is no shame in being a manager. God made some to be managers and some to be visionaries. Managers have beneficial qualities visionaries don't and vice versa. But being a manager doesn't mean you can't tweak a ministry to keep pace with social norms and remain equipped to address the problems those norms bring with them.

Membership Focus: *What are you, a manager or a visionary?*

Don't strive to be something you are not merely because one or the other is the standard model promoted in our culture or your church. Word of warning: managers generally don't get the celebrity status bestowed on visionaries. Don't let that tempt you to declare yourself a visionary if you are a manager.

Is the Sacred Really Sacred

Paper, Paste & Ink – Let's zoom in on this idea of the sacred. I want to recount a real-life experience as an example. When I was a young teen, my parents were spring cleaning and gave my brother and me a box of periodicals to burn (Yes! We could burn trash in our back yard in those days). Among those periodicals were a bunch of old Sunday school quarterlies. Because they regarded spiritual matters, we ranked them up there with the Bible and saw them as sacred in our child's minds. Being very reticent to burn them, my brother questioned my parents about it before we proceeded with Fahrenheit 451 (Bradbury, 1953).

That brings us to our next prayer pointer.

<u>**Key Insight for Prayer:**</u> Be careful about what you hold sacred and don't hold sacred. Clinging to the wrong things as sacred can derail you from advancing to greater heights. Another way of looking at this is to discern what is negotiable and nonnegotiable.

Legends Aren't Sacred – But Can be Respected – Many in your church may deem the prayer program sacred, established by a spiritual giant under a directive from God. But now, that founder has passed down through the annals of founding archetypes of the faith in your congregation. So, we memorialize them by defending the prayer ministry's status quo out of respect for their foundational efforts. I'm about 99% certain that the founder would disagree with that course of action simply because founders generally don't see themselves as legends. I think they would subscribe to what I'm about to present.

As humans, we haven't arrived (Eph 4:13b); therefore, our journey (e.g., the prayer program) should be in a constant state of moving forward. In other words, the prayer program established in time immemorial by the now exalted pioneer prayer warrior...............is not sacred. It needs to progress onto greater heights, just as Abram did. If Abram saw God's communiqué as hallowed, he would have built a temple in Haran on the basis that he overlooked the contents of the communiqué as sacred. This frame of mind is very much in line with a humorous illustration of a child receiving a gift. In her excitement, she carefully and methodically removes the pretty wrapping, throws the gift away, and keeps the wrapping.

Membership Focus: *To be realistic, if you feel the existing program is adequate and it's not necessary to try and improve upon it at this time, then stop there. The danger here is over-engineering and making the prayer group an end in itself and not the means to an end.*

Gideon's Army – Let me touch on a prayer scenario that should help us differentiate between what is sacred and what is not. In my estimation, the jury is still out on the practice of having these 24-hour prayer vigils. In these vigils, people come to the church at specific time slots throughout the day and night to pray for a particular need brought to the congregation's attention. To me, that smacks of trying to look sacrificially spiritual, primarily because I consider it unnecessary. I see the so-called sacrifice as more artificial than genuine. It runs a grave risk of appearing like the Pharisee in Luke 18, who went up to the Temple to pray alongside a tax collector. I might be so bold as to say promoting an ordered prayer schedule for the church at large is less effective than heartfelt petitions from a few. That said, the invitation can and should go out to the entire church body, but there need not be any time constraints. Schedule it for the middle of the night or the middle of the day. It doesn't matter; just don't get cutesy or gimmicky with bells and whistles.

I guess I'm not clear as to why Gideon's army is irrelevant here. That's sarcasm; Gideon's army is very relevant here. It's not a sacrifice if the prayer vigil is for display. Many people may show up just because of the corporate excitement generated by the prayer vigil's proponents. The funny thing is when you show up at 3:30 AM, there is no one there, and that spirit of corporate excitement is somewhat lacking. I know because I was one of those. As I recall, I signed up for the 2:30 AM slot, but still, no one was there. However, in defense of the prayer vigil, with no one there to witness my "sacrifice," it made me question whether I was there for the right reason.

Whatever happened to going to your prayer closet and getting face down where no one can see you? If you want to sacrifice without display, I'm not sure how you do that since the act of *wanting* to implies you are disingenuous about it in the first place. If you feel the need to hold a vigil, then mobilize those in the church congregation who are willing to engage in a time of prayer in the evening time. If it happens, let it drift into the wee hours of the morning with no appointed end time. If people can't show up until late, and that extends the prayer vigil throughout the night, so be

Life Event Number 3 - Abraham

it. But beyond scheduling a start time to assemble for corporate prayer, don't over-schedule it.

Maybe I'm splitting hairs on semantics but at this juncture, let me distinguish between what I perceive as *wanting* to and *willing* to sacrifice. Genuine sacrifice focuses on the issue or the recipient, not the one making the sacrifice. Hence, the person willing to sacrifice focuses less on themselves and more on the recipient. Any emphasis on themselves centers on how they can effectively accomplish their task, not how sacrificial they are. In other words, they don't say things like, "I canceled an event to be here, so let's get started."

They may not even see their action as a sacrifice. Were the costs even counted? Of course, they were, but the person willing to sacrifice deemed the costs worth it. Furthermore, they neither seek credit nor want others to credit them. So, the willingness is inherently divorced from the desire to be praised or placed on a pedestal. Don't confuse wanting to pray with wanting to sacrifice. *Wanting* to pray is akin to being *willing* to sacrifice, which is others-centered, not self-centered.

I'm in favor of the scriptural maxim *"where two or more gather in my name."* But don't let the "more" compel you to go to the extreme of overhyping a prayer vigil. My concern is that having an official church-sanctioned event runs the risk of shaming people into caring enough to do something about it. If having to reorder your priorities to attend a prayer vigil is an annoying inconvenience, something is wrong. Aside from the few who care, the remaining participants may be ambivalent and participate just because they are "supposed to," not because they want to. Or they may be more concerned about how it will reflect on them if they don't show up. Either of these latter two reasons is essentially for show.

Additionally, prayer vigils implicitly foster the misconception that God responds in direct proportion to the number of people who participate versus the number of people who genuinely care. My question is, what threshold number of passive participants is required before God responds? Are we to believe that we can't count on the five prayer team members, so we need to recruit 500 to get God to sit up and take notice? If you want to rally 50 or 1000 people to a prayer rally, that's not wrong, per se, but don't be disappointed if it doesn't have the results you intended or hoped it would have. Succinctly stated, don't equate expectations with participation. I suppose the counter-argument is if only the five prayer team members care, what then?

So, despite all of the pitfalls I've pointed out about prayer vigils, can we identify any instances in which we should hold a church Sponsored prayer vigil? One example is if the issue is global enough that it causes most people in the church to sit up and take notice. The term global would refer to any situation inside or outside the church that will significantly impact the church. Closing out this discussion with Gideon's army, people's willingness to sacrifice will be manifest in the number that shows up and the length of time they stay. Remember the Master-slave Principle. The act of praying is the Master, the vigil, and how it plays out is the slave.

So here is our applicable prayer pointer

Key Insight for Prayer: pray that God would instill an attitude of sacrifice in the hearts of your church members – not a mentality, but an attitude.

Unwinding the Wound – Now, suppose your existing prayer program is mediocre. The reason may be because we as humans like to program a program to run on its own (that's why they call it a program). Our objective is to wind it up, let it go, and never worry about it again. But you, a new upstart prayer warrior, come along, and you feel the need to upset the apple cart. You see the current system as being on life support, and everyone is just going through the motions. You know those little old ladies I mentioned above that were part of the prayer group before you were born. They are probably the very ones who would like to see someone like you come along and breathe some life into it. These little old lady prayer warriors have a better sense of the church's pulse than most, and they know how the prayer group is doing. They are bastions of stoic wisdom who impart that wisdom only to those who have ears to hear – maybe you.

Coming Full Circle – So, let's close the loop on your beginnings. I like closing loops. Your second level is to get the other prayer warriors passionate about making a course correction. Of course, you need to have a game plan because no one likes a rabble-rouser that doesn't have a plan. Don't stir the pot and walk away, expecting them to take the baton when it was your idea in the first place. Remember, however, at this point, you are a trusted member of the church, and so they will be more likely to listen to you.

Also, you may be shocked to know that they would like for you to lead the group since you appear to be willing to take responsibility. Many people don't want to take on responsibility in ministries. They are eager to tag along and participate. But, they don't feel confident enough to shoulder the burden of success. Now, while true, that is strictly a humanistic way of looking at it. In reality, if no one is willing to step up to the plate and lead, then God probably has not called them to lead – or at least they have not been willing to acknowledge His call. Alternatively, they may well be the Abrams that declined God's calling. That may be why you feel drawn to answer His call. So that is how you begin at the beginning when you jump into the middle.

With that, let's revisit our previous prayer pointer on the sacred and add one:

Key Insight for Prayer:

1. Pray for discernment of what is sacred and what is not – another way of looking at this is to discern what is negotiable and nonnegotiable.
2. Pray for vision and innovative ideas on implementing these visions in a manner compatible with God's master plan.

Everything is Optional

Choice is a Choice – I want to return to the binary principle of choice. That is the one element of control God has fully vested in us. Now don't get too excited, because as noted above, we have freedom of choice, but we do not have freedom of consequences. We all know what happened with Sarai's decision to hand over Hagar as a surrogate. We'll talk further about that later. As it relates to Abraham (and Noah before him), no one held a gun to his head and made him leave his home and his people. While he was en route, he could have chosen to turn around at any time and go home. So, unless someone is holding a gun to your head, no one is holding a gun to your head.

I have another story for you, a true-life story, I might add, of a professor handing out a difficult assignment to his students. Someone unclear on the concept groaned and asked, "Dr. H., do we really have to do this?" The professor responded with his characteristic grin and light-hearted tone, "Everything is optional; you don't have to do a thing."

How does choice relate to our beginnings as well as every step along our journey? I will preface my response with a few questions. How much of a fatalist are you? Do you believe God so orchestrates our lives that the pathway and destination set for your church is assured? Do you think your participation is not required for your church to arrive at its destination? If so, that is not entirely accurate, but I will give a qualified concurrence. The assurance of your church's success can only result from someone making the initial choice to believe. That someone must then followed up by electing to obey every step of the way. In other words, for a church's success to be assured, God **will** find His Abram, who **will** submit.

We Imprison Ourselves – Let's recast the same principle in a negative context. If we believe our church's fate conforms to the typical life cycle of birth, growth, peak, decline, and death, there is one of two disorders afflicting us. One is that we are unwilling to think outside the confines of our circumstances. The other is that we fear the consequences of failure if we choose to step out on faith with the intent of disrupting the life cycle process. The latter case becomes a self-fulfilled prophecy. Generally, when we fear the consequences, we don't believe that God is able or willing. I add the caveat that the latter may materialize if the leadership chooses to establish their church's destiny and course. That is, God may not be willing to ensure our success if the pastor and elders choose a destination or pathway contrary to God's. As part of my reinforcing argument to the earlier quote, *"Early sparks of faith"* are tested at this decision point. Fail the test, and you will never know what could have been; pass the test, and you will *"increase your faith for things on down the road."*

Life Event Number 3 - Abraham

As I noted earlier, we tend to impose our limitations on God so that we really *can't* believe that He is able. Now don't confuse this with earlier key insights about taking baby steps to start a ministry. In that context, I was targeting our limitations. In the current context, I'm targeting the imposition of our limits onto a limitless God. In this latter context, we believe that the forces of nature and society trump God every time. For this reason, the choices we make on the direction to take our church are typically based on logistical or financial constraints and not on whether God is in it or not.

Here is an excellent place to address the question of whether our resource limitations are imposed by God or by our lack of faith in stepping up to bigger things. If resources are God Imposed, He has provided financing for the scope of work He intends at that stage, not the vision we may have received. If the latter, God may limit funding due to our lack of faith. Again, God **can** do it without us, but He **won't** do it without us. Unfortunately, in cases where the church body is weak in faith, we tend to veil it in the guise of whether our pastor is a good fundraiser, not whether we have faith. It is a dynamic tug-of-war that is a function of our collective relationship with God.

If, in the one extreme, we are content to be a church of the status quo or of "me and mine and no one else," then it's probably not a good idea to step out on faith. Likely, God will not bless us with resources beyond our operating expenses. It's not that He is punitive or stingy. It's just that God will not waste His resources on someone's unilateral plan that is not in line with His grand strategy for the community. In this, the leadership may, quite frankly, be completely unaware. In the opposite extreme, we may be eager to charge Hell with a squirt gun and only require that God give us unlimited resources. In that case, it's still not a good idea to step out on faith. God is not likely to trust us with resources that we will squander on boondoggle ministry efforts that He never authorized. Both extremes are illegitimate exercises of early sparks of faith. Recall what happened to the Israelites when they decided to launch an assault on the Promised Land after God told them to return to the desert. It didn't exactly work out well because God revoked their authorization to take the Promised Land when they decided it was impossible to conquer.

When we are in the optimal position of walking in lockstep with God, we pursue only those ministries He has called us to take on. That is when we step out in faith beyond our means – a legitimate exercise of early sparks of faith. So, the tug-of-war is really within ourselves and not with God. That's one of those human conditions that the Asian proverb succinctly describes, "We carry our prison within ourselves." In this case, our prison is our fear of failure.

Membership Focus: *So, at this point, I'm asking you to do two things:*

1. *Address your **crisis of belief** and come to grips with the question of whether you believe God is able and*
2. *Discern which way God wants you to jump and then jump without fear of consequences or failure.*

Mountains into Molehills – The problem is that perceived failures, or imminent failures may only be obstacles that loom as insurmountable barriers. These so-called barriers hinder our ability to believe and act on that belief. By way of an oblique application to this struggle, Jesus said, *this kind does not go out except by prayer and fasting* (Matt. 17:21). The context of that passage is a demon-possessed boy. However, the basic principle undergirding this passage involves our spiritual battle against opposing forces, whether demonic or human.

In our situation, confidently discerning God's direction may only come with prayer and fasting. Otherwise, you are not just walking blind practically, but you are also walking blind spiritually. In other words, you can't see your path logistically if you can't see it spiritually. Once you are confident of God's will, failures will diminish to *surmountable* obstacles you can step over or paper tigers you can crash through. Once you know God's will, the right choices will be clear – obstacles will be things you look beyond. Poor choices come from uncertainty on what God's will is. So, don't hinder your progress with the baggage of poor decisions. As Hebrews' writer says, *lay aside every weight and the sin which so easily ensnares us* (Hebrews 12:1).

Faith Indicator – On the flip side, however, we can certainly choose not to make spiritual progress if we make the wrong choices. My husband had a Taiwanese professor who expressed this concept as follows, "If you end up being a shoe salesman, you should be happy because that is what you worked for." In my discipline, the well-known psychologist, William Glasser, said, "Behavior is a choice." Although both quotes are from secular sources, there's real wisdom in both expressions, and the proponents expressed the concept well. Glasser was not the first one to discover this principle. The entire Bible contains real-life accounts of individuals who made wise, godly choices. It also tells of many tales of woe and sin-sick souls who chose very unwisely. Remember what I said about how spiritual principles intertwine? Our choices are faith indicators. It tells what you genuinely believe. Henry Blackaby said, "How you live your life is a testimony of what you believe about God" (1990).

If you elect not to step out on faith, you either don't have faith, or your fear of failure suffocates your early sparks of faith.

Foundations Require Crushed Stone – Hopefully, your church is traveling down a road paved with good choices. Hopefully, you are staying on track by incorporating God's word into your hearts and lives. In so doing, being sensitive listeners to the Word, and above all else, heeding it (Jas 1: 23-25). Sadly, however, not all churches are characterized this way. We will all experience some failure and defeat in our journey! Our fallen nature will see to that. Praise God, though! Our new character can intervene. It can press us on to victory, but we need to learn how to appropriate it. Note, I said "can press us on," not "will press us on." *And this is the victory that has overcome the world – our faith.* (1st Jn 5:4-5).

Membership Focus: *If you are experiencing failure, despite getting off to an exciting start, or if the fate of all you worked for appears to be in jeopardy, despair not. Rather persevere! "Failures, repeated failures, are finger posts on the road to achievement. One fails forward toward success" (C. S. Lewis, 1952).*

Failure is part of the foundation of trials we must experience and work through in our walk. That is what I discussed under Noah. Failures could be God's way of instilling the right way of doing things, not because they are His perfect will, but because He uses them to bring good out of failure. That is what God does. So, if we find ourselves in an endless do-loop of "try, try again," it may be that we are kicking against the goads and refusing to believe that we are doing it the wrong way.

Life Event Number 3 - Abraham

There is one prayer pointer we can draw out of this.

Key Insight for Prayer: Pray that your church develops a sensitivity to God's leading to choose what stimulates growth. Pray that no failure would be in vain, but God would bring victory out of disappointment.

Oh, I never finished my anecdote about the class assignment. Did I mention that all the students understood they would have gotten a zero for that assignment had they taken Dr. H up on his offer? Freedom of choice, not freedom of consequences.

Story Time

Regarding small beginnings, let me return to my story about the mission church I spoke of earlier. It's the story of a group of very dedicated Christians who began a church in Cypress, TX, the second campus for a large church in northwest Houston. They are a sterling example of faith and patience for starting a brand-new work in a brand-new community. For three years, they met in a school cafeteria. These Cypress pioneers believed in God for a campus and church building of their own.

Every Sunday, this faithful band of believers had the back-breaking and tedious task of setting up and tearing down. They unloaded and set up tables and chairs to give the school cafeteria an appearance of a worship center. This same congregation had to remove all the desks, tables, and chairs in the school classrooms in preparation for their small groups. Then they had to restore everything to its original condition before leaving for the day. The stage also had to be made ready for the praise team that was leading worship. And, of course, the musicians had the laborious

Life Event Number 3 - Abraham

responsibility of unloading, setting up, tearing down, and reloading all their sound equipment every single Lord's Day.

Imagine how monotonous this must have been Sunday after Sunday! Yet, they remained faithful from the beginning until the day their new campus opened for ~~business~~ worship. The Cypress pioneers were only able to do it because they adopted a patient attitude and a life of prayer.

Key Insight for Prayer: Pray that the laity would forge ahead even in the face of drudgery and monotony.

So, you have been pushing hard to launch your new ministry, and for what level of success you have achieved, you have the satisfaction of a job well done. After a successful beginning, or after achieving milestones on the way, what do you like to do? Yes! Celebrate! Not only should your congregation celebrate, but you and your prayer warriors should celebrate. Celebration rejuvenates and recharges the spirit to forge on.

So, celebrate your small accomplishments.

That was not a prayer pointer.

Small beginnings are just the prelude to the end goal God has set for your church. They are milestones along the road to success. You'll never really appreciate the wonder and joy of these spectacular moments until you've learned how to celebrate your small accomplishments. Look for them all along the way! When you understand how far you've come since the beginning, it will encourage you to keep on. It will help you stay focused on your goal. It will generate praise in your daily walk and create an attitude of thanksgiving in your heart (Zech. 4:10 (NIV): *Who dares despise the day of small things...*). When our son was just a baby and learning how to walk, we were so thrilled to see his first steps. He would giggle with delight at each small step he took. That's the way it is with our Christian walk. You must be patient and progress at a rate that doesn't exceed your capacity to advance.

Guideline Wrap Up: Casting the Past into the Future

Let's pause and list the salient points of what small beginnings do for us. Our prayers should accompany each of these points to make a God thing out of them.

Small beginnings:

1. Teach us humility.
2. Teach us dependence upon God as our provider, the source of all good things, and all our blessings
3. Produce godly character,
4. Cause us to celebrate life – not taking anything for granted, and
5. Stimulate your church's faith.

Looking back upon your small beginnings will strengthen your faith for future endeavors, which God has set for you to do. That is another reinforcing point for the quote, *"Early sparks of faith will serve as our example of how you can increase your faith for things on down the road."* An implied application of this quote relates to those reluctant to move out in the first place. The perceived enormity of the task ahead can squelch early sparks of faith. As such, early steps of faith are not easy but are necessary!

Membership Focus: *If this is the case for you or anyone you know, here is my counsel. Don't look at the mountain. Look at the* *foothills of the task, and when you conquer the foothills, look back to see how far you have come.* Not only will this encourage you to go forward, but the mountain doesn't look so formidable—especially since you may be halfway to the peak by this point. *This aspect of looking back is primarily for those who are timid or reluctant to move out independently. To all others who feel they are in a race, the standard counsel is not to look back.*

<u>Key Insight for Prayer:</u> Pray that fellow saints will not falter at the task's enormity but be encouraged by the distance they have already come.

What can we say of Abraham in these small beginnings? He was content to follow his Lord one day at a time and one step at a time. He let God chart his course and determine his progress. Abraham knew deep in his heart that somehow, someway, he and Sarah would eventually arrive at their destination. So, it seems we've transitioned from our discussion on small beginnings and into one on faith. That brings us to the following guideline, which, as noted above, is inextricably interwoven with Guideline #5 on small beginnings.

Guideline #6 – Begin with Obedience – Do Not Stifle Your Faith

<u>Applicability</u>

- **Target Populations:** This has the same multilevel applicability
    1. Your church body as an entity
    2. Any ministry spawned by your church body, and

3. The rank and file church member

Hebrew 11:8: ***By faith, Abraham obeyed*** *when he was called to go out to the place which he would receive as an inheritance. And he went out, not knowing where he was going.*

And again,

Hebrew 11:17: ***By faith*** *Abraham, when he was tested, offered up Isaac, and he who had received the promises offered up his only begotten son [in obedience], (brackets added)*

and finally

Romans 6:16: *Do you not know that to whom you present yourselves slaves to obey, you are that one's slaves whom you obey, whether of sin leading to death, or of obedience leading to righteousness?*

Topical Delineation and Elaboration

Begin with faith and absolute confidence in God. Abram kept right on trusting the Lord in the *limitations* of his small beginnings. And amid these small beginnings, God taught him so much about the merits of faith and obedience. Someone once said that faith is what lies on the other side of your dreams. The scriptures bear this out repeatedly. There is probably not a single central figure in Genesis that doesn't support this premise. Abram trusted the Lord to materialize the vision placed in his mind and heart. And Abram is the one to whom God imparted righteousness because of his faith.

Now there are two facets to Abram's faith. One involves his destination; the other involves his progeny. Let's touch on the first facet.

Abram's Destiny

Trust Me – God told him to leave his father's land and journey to a place *He would disclose to him later*. That undisclosed location meant that God had not told him exactly where he was going. It did not mean a place Abram never heard of before. We know he knew of Canaan because that's where Terah and his family were heading before they got waylaid in Haran. It's just that Abram didn't know that Canaan was where God was taking him. Why the mystery if that is where Abram was going in the first place? It's a mystery because it forced Abram to believe, to have faith.

Do you think Abram would have shown as much faith if God had told him Canaan was his destination? Or do you think Abram would have exhibited as much faith if God allowed Terah to be the vehicle for getting Abram to Canaan? Terah would have been the central figure; Abram would have only been a tag along. As it was, Abram either had to exhibit belief by departing on his own or tell God, "Thanks, I think I'll pass." So, Abram had to demonstrate faith before the journey even began. Not to beat a dead horse, but again, "Early sparks of faith…".

Hypothetically speaking, what if Abram would have told God, "I don't know about this; let me count the costs and weigh the pros and cons first." Have you ever wondered how many scores of people throughout history walked away from God's calling because they lacked faith in God's ability to provide? Or they honestly believed their inadequacy was a legitimate obstacle to God? I hyperbolized this last statement in jest because we are all guilty of that. In this regard, let's touch on the aspect of *"a lack of faith."* That is the default position we always take in explaining why someone fails to answer God's call or respond to an open door with a limited window of opportunity.

Different Viewpoint, Different End Point – I want to take a different tact on this idea of "a lack of faith," and I want to approach it with a question. Why in the world would God call us to do anything if we lacked faith or were devoid of belief – and He knew it? We talked earlier about a crisis of faith; this question puts us in a contradiction of faith. That is, stepping out on something we don't have (i.e., faith) is a contradiction. At best, we can claim God tests people to see if they will step out on faith, but it's not a test if they lack that quality. Without going into a protracted discussion on the ramifications of this question, let's skip that conversation and go straight to the answer. The answer is He wouldn't. I don't think God calls anyone to task if they don't believe. And I don't think we are devoid of it. It's my conviction that we enter this world equipped with an infantile degree of faith, just like we come into this world equipped with a love for God and with a sense of the spiritual realm. Again, all this is part and parcel of being created in His image. However, I think we suppress the faith we have in making our choices. We squelch our faith through our obsession with walking by sight.

Early sparks of faith cannot become a flame of faith without it being testing or exercised. So, when God does test our faith, the test will be within our capacity to believe, but it's our choice as to whether we step out to exercise that faith. Can I rephrase the question above? Have you ever wondered how many scores of people throughout history walked away from God's calling due to a fear of stepping out on faith? And as a result, they smothered the belief they did have in God's ability to provide?

Do you see where this takes us? By rephrasing the question, I'm shifting the responsibility to me. I'm transferring it from the excuse *"it's not my fault"* to the confession *"it is my fault."* I'm reassigning the blame from *"circumstances beyond my control"* to *"circumstances within my control."* I am placing accountability squarely on myself, the person God is calling to step out on faith. It may be our perception that God did not gift us with the ability to believe, but that's not true. It only becomes a *lack of faith* when it is *unexercised* or *quashed*. So, when I use the phrase *"lack of faith,"* please interpret it as deliberately stifled faith.

Membership Focus: *Simply receiving a calling from God does not guarantee success on our part. We choose **not** to make spiritual progress when we decide **not** to step out. Don't let that be you or your church.*

A More Powerful Force – I honestly think we don't know what a potent force faith is. If you think about it, there is not a single moment in our lives when we don't place the total weight of trust in our circumstances. Being physically able to do something is how we typically gauge our willingness to do that something. But there is a more powerful force than being physically capable. Yes! The willingness aspect. Everything you do is because you believe you have control over the outcome and deem it positive. Conversely, everything we choose not to do is because we believe a positive end is not guaranteed. So, faith is the ever-present driver in our lives, not the physical ability to get up and do something.

Once we believe, only then can we proceed through the various facets of our journey to our destination – your development depends on it. Our destiny, the end product we develop into, comprises a life of experiences and lessons learned.

Abram's Progeny

Cutting Ties or Against All Odds – Let's move on to the second facet of faith, Abram's progeny. The *idea* of leaving home and the *idea* of making Abram a great nation are tied together. We'll start with the promise to make him a great nation. Let's conservatively assume that implied is the understanding it is through family and tribal lines. Well, it is, but Abram didn't know that, and he didn't have the luxury of thinking along common-sense lines like these. Nor was there any implied understanding that Abram would round up a loose confederation of nomads and develop a great nation from that.

Since Sarai was barren when God called him, that cut off the family line resource. And having left behind what family he had in Chaldea cut off the extended family resource. They knew all that when God called him. At that point, Abram would have had to believe God against all odds to move from his homeland to an unknown destination. So, what is the principle here? Faith *must* defy human reasoning. A commonsense assertion, but one we typically believe applies to the other fellow – not us.

Thus far, we have two lessons of faith:

1. it must precede action and
2. it must defy human reasoning.

But You Promised! – But "Say," you ask, "didn't he get a little bit off track with Hagar, which kind of negates any claim to faith on his part?" Yes, he did, as he took Hagar to be a surrogate wife. From our viewpoint, it appears that Abram was a passive participant in the decision-making process for this set of actions. As

I read the scripture, he took Hagar as his concubine because Sarai <u>said so</u> – and that settled it.

As an alternative explanation, I believe the miscue lay in Abram's *interpretation* of what God promised! For that promise to come to pass, Abram had to have a male heir. But precisely what did God promise – that Abram and Sarai would have a biological child of their own? As far as scripture goes, when God first called him, He never told Abram who would have his children or how many there would be. Logic would dictate that Sarai would bear him a son. That particular line of reasoning, however, goes out the window if Sarai is barren. It wasn't until after Abram arrived in Canaan as a sojourner that God told him that *his seed* would inherit the land (Gen. 12:7).

So, a lot of sand had blown over the dunes before God told Abram it would be through his family line. That's great for Abram; it doesn't say much for Sarai. That is, God still doesn't say Sarai would be the mother. So hypothetically speaking, it could have been Hagar. It wasn't until after Abram had his run-in with Pharaoh and Lot parted company (even more sand over the dunes) that God said Sarai would be the mother. You will remember, when God finally did say Sarah would bear Abraham a son, it caught her by surprise – big time (Genesis 18:9-12). No doubt her response was, "why am I always the last to know?" To you and me, that's only about two chapters, but to Abraham, that was maybe two decades. Considering this set of circumstances, we should probably go easy on the couple since God's promise was something way outside the norm. Given that most of us probably couldn't have done any better, it's hard to fault Abram for his lapse of faith.

According to Who's Reckoning?

Hindsight Morality – Let's run a little further with this idea of a righteous Abram falling victim to an unrighteous moral transgression because that seems to trip us up perpetually. We understand the motivation; we get it, but there is something about the conventional answer that nags at the back of my mind. It just doesn't seem to answer the issue altogether. Otherwise, we wouldn't keep bringing it up. Let's sidestep the aspect of their motivation and approach it from the question of why Abram and Sarai thought they had permission, if you will, to go through with their backup plan.

I have found that people are bound or loosed by their cultural customs. These customs encompass matters as small as proper etiquette to issues as central as moral standards. What we find acceptable in our culture may be unacceptable in a foreign culture. What we might find objectionable in our present-day culture might be conventional in ancient cultures. Is there a cultural custom we've missed that would help us understand this affair without necessarily condoning it? For the moment, try and accept the premise that what Abram and Hagar did may not have been considered wrong from their viewpoint. On what basis can I legitimately justify this position? On two bases, actually. On the first basis, I'll let the Apostle Paul respond: *For until the law sin was in the world, but sin is not imputed when there is no law* (Romans 5:13). That doesn't mean there wasn't any law of the land; it just means God had not handed down His version of the law yet. And to be sure, there is the law of conscience that God has instilled in us all. But as you know, we are quite capable of manipulating written laws to salve a guilty conscience.

Life Event Number 3 - Abraham

On the second basis, I'll let Abram and Sarai provide the answer I would have expected them to give. The law of the land I reference above is the written code of Hammurabi, extant in Abram's day. That code expressly permitted this practice. It was not an interpretation; the code spelled it out. It states that the first wife would receive the child on her lap as a symbolic gesture that the child is hers (Bibleview.org). So, it appears that it was in full accord with Hammurabi's moral codes. Abram and Sarai were likely far more familiar with and *comfortable* with Hammurabi's code than anything God had conveyed to them up to that point. That is, they were acting on a standard they did know as opposed to a standard they did not know, i.e., God's standard and, by extension, our convention. As a side note, that may give an enormous clue as to why God honored Abram's request to bless his progeny through Ishmael. Keep letting Paul's statement drum through your head.

Isn't choosing to be born thousands of years later great? We can look back and impose all sorts of hindsight principles and present-day ethical codes on Abram. So why the prolonged digression on Abram's moral lapse? Well, this detour wasn't a detour; it has relevance on how to pray for our churches. I will touch on that a few paragraphs from now. For now, I want to wind up our discussion on Abram and Sarai trying to find hope in a pathway of hopelessness.

I Think We May Have it Backwards – In hindsight, it's easy to stand firm in the belief that Abram and Sarai believed God would swoop in about 25 years later and change things. Let's bring it back to earth now and put ourselves in Sarai's sandals. From a human standpoint, the inability to alter her physiological condition, much less interrupt the process, is nothing short of miraculous. Sarai viewed her barrenness as effectively cast in stone. Scripture indicates she believed it **was** of the Lord (Genesis 16:2), so who among us is remotely justified to reprimand her for her decision. We can't expect her to believe that God would allow her to have a child in contradiction of a decree she fervently believed He mandated. We might make that interpretation in retrospect, but we can't expect her to make that interpretation. Viewing it in this context should give us a hint of the vast disconnect between the reality of her barrenness and a distant hope that God had instilled in their hearts. But because we know the end of the story, we can't possibly comprehend the full impact of that disconnect on Abram and Sarai. So, we tend to cast it in terms that God chose Abram because he was a man of tremendous faith and a significant figure in Israel's history. In reality, Abram was a nobody, and he became a man of immense faith because God forged it into him. It should cause us to realize that God can even use "me" to accomplish His objective. It should cause us to want to believe God for a miracle.

Membership Focus: *Speaking of wanting to, does God want to interrupt your daily existence with a blessing? The predisposition of the Father to touch our personal life, our family's lives, or the family of God with a miracle awaits even us.*

Membership Focus: *Oh yes, there's more. The process of fertility begs another question. What infertile ground does God want to break up in your church? Spawning any new ministry in your church or even jumpstarting your church is a form of reproduction, and fertilization is necessary for reproduction. As humans, we do not have the reproductive capabilities to accomplish either of these. Nor do we need to understand what is in store for us or what God has planned for us. Only God needs to know, and only a touch from God can do that. We just need to be receptive.*

Only One Thing God Asks of You – It wasn't until after this debacle with Hagar that God told Abram otherwise. Abram and Sarai had not realized the full depth of God's promises to them. But they didn't need to understand it; God didn't condition it on the expectation that they must think outside the box on something that was beyond their comprehension. The proof is that God was indeed faithful in keeping his promise to this duo despite their weak faith and lack of foresight. They had a wonderful biological son, Isaac, with no help from a surrogate. The extraordinary thing about this is that Abraham was 100 years old, and Sarah was 90 years old when Isaac was born.

Insofar as meeting God's expectations, He only expected one thing of Abram – to believe (Romans 4:3). Period. End of statement. He didn't expect Abram to understand; God just asked him to believe what He revealed to him up to that point. Remember the discussion on Noah and his purpose? Abram's purpose was to believe. That's all.

Membership Focus: *We don't need to know how God will do it, only that He will do it.*

What is Your Norm? – Here is where I return to the subject of Abram's moral lapse, but I'm going the bring it into the present day and spin it differently. Looking back on the churches I grew up in during the mid-20th century, they were good evangelical churches. That means their primary focus was birthing new believers. I can bear them witness that their focus was a legitimate drive and not a numbers game. If this were a conversation between members of one of those churches, they would have said, "Praise the Lord! I just love seeing lost souls come to the Lord." Nothing is wrong with that, but none of us knew what to do after that except congratulation them and say we look forward to seeing them in church next week. Succinctly put, they (we) were passionate about winning the lost with little idea of how to follow up. Kind of like driving our car off a cliff and wondering, "now what?" In one of our guest speaking venues, the visiting pastor reprimanded the evangelical church (and us by inclusion) for our practice of treating soul-winning as an end in itself. That is, we win a soul to Christ, and our job is done. Paraphrasing, he said it is equivalent to tossing a newborn baby on the bed and saying, "live baby." The implication is that we had a severe problem in our neglect of discipleship.

The evangelical churches I grew up in were teaching centers that taught us spiritual truths and doctrine. They did that well, but their acme was not necessarily discipleship. Do you see the difference? They taught academic knowledge, not practicing knowledge. The few times they did teach "how-to" classes, they pertained to soul-winning. I would go so far as to say they equated instruction with discipleship. I attribute that to an unconscious belief that righteous, moral living is easily achieved in your own strength because now you were a Christian – voila!

There is nothing wrong with academic knowledge; it's a noble pursuit. But in all this teaching, the call to a faith walk or an invitation to ministry seemed subordinate to the unspoken expectation to be an upstanding church member or a moral person. Perhaps intrinsic to our church culture was the underlying mentality that we could achieve holiness by striving to be righteous. And the concept of obedience? Outside of the mantra of being "obedient to the faith through baptism," I don't recall the pastor emphasizing obedience as an integral part of the Christian Walk. Perhaps I have a poor memory, but that was my perception. I do remember that classes were continually on the docket. While the intent was to equip us better, taking more courses on this topic or that topic was a great way of avoiding any ministry outside the church walls. In other words, someone in good conscience could follow a path designed to lead toward ministry and subvert it to evade that endpoint. While we might agree that this is not a healthy approach for the Christian walk, would you go so far as to say it was morally wrong? Abram and Sarai thought their Plan B was satisfactory; we believe it was not. We consider our church customs to be honorable. Are they?

Now I absolutely believe we should live moral lives and have high ethical expectations for Christians. Yet, my generation's unspoken mindset was that righteous and virtuous living were the primary goals we were to strive for – not faith and obedience.

So, I've drawn what I perceive is a subtle distinction between the Christian walk as it was and what it should have been. Perhaps your perception isn't the same. Maybe you see the difference as glaring? I ask again, do you believe that neglecting discipleship in pursuit of doctrinal knowledge is acceptable, unacceptable, or neutral? Was what Abram and Hagar did right, wrong, or neutral? It depends on your culture. Is that not true?

Here is the application. Our churches follow practices which "feel right" because they are modeled and promoted as acceptable by those who preceded us. In the case of my church experience, I would submit that knowledge without discipleship borders on a transgression against the believer. Yet, none of us considered it wrong; we thought it was an honorable pursuit. But just because we believed it was discipleship doesn't mean we were being discipled. The passage of scripture that supports my argument is 1st

Corinthians 8:1b *Knowledge puffs up, but love edifies.* Would you not agree that acquiring greater love is the objective of discipleship?

Despite my belief that our 20th-century approach was lopsided in favor of evangelism and instruction, no one intentionally defrauded us, as it were. I benefited from that knowledge and the general worship environment, but here is where we hit a dead end. I could not duplicate that in anyone. To my recollection, no instructional opportunities were available that would have equipped me to disciple someone else. And there were no mature Christians equipped to disciple me or others of my immaturity. Were we then defrauded unintentionally? Perhaps. My mother would say, "Honey, you can't draw from an empty well." Without reservation, our leaders went to extraordinary lengths to provide us with what they believed to be the best. What was missing? Somewhere in our history leading up to the present-day culture, we lost the skill of mentoring those coming up behind us. We drifted into a mentality that everyone is responsible for navigating their path through life. I think it's a byproduct of "personal rights," which has become ingrained into our culture. All of what I just described was second nature to us. It was desirable, honorable, and sufficient. But it wasn't sufficient; we just believed it was. So, just as Hammurabi's code was probably second nature to Abram and Sarai, our church culture is second nature to us.

The global application here is that Abram's lapse was not considered wrong to him and Sarai, but it was a drag on his mission and calling. By extension, teaching biblical principles without discipleship was not wrong in our sight, but it stunted our growth. At best, it was moderately beneficial to our spiritual growth. At worst, it was detrimental by making us think we were growing in Christ when we were only increasing in knowledge.

Membership Focus: *Are you beginning to realize why we can't place blind trust in our cultural norms? Are you starting to understand that we need to question what we may be neglecting out of ignorance? What customs can you pinpoint in your church that no one considers wrong but may well be detrimental to believers and particularly new believers? What common perceptions have become ingrained in your belief system that may be acting as dead weights on your ability to soar spiritually? Are new believers unintentionally defrauded because seasoned church members honestly think they are doing the right thing by perpetuating dead-weight beliefs and customs?*

Let me now swing to the opposite side of the issue. I can attest that the churches I grew up in definitely did not teach legalism. The idea of a faith walk was just not an overt guiding principle. It may have been there, but it was either understood or implied but not overtly expressed. I think there was simply an expectation that we would all achieve moral, righteous lives through osmosis from education and corporate worship. I know this because it was a real eye-opener when Roy Hession came to speak at our church, and I bought his book, "Not I but Christ" (1980). The title pretty much tells the story of how we can't live holy or moral lives in our strength.

While the above discussion on discipleship is a lesson in itself, it was not my point; it was only the vehicle to make my point. My focus was to emphasize righteousness through obedience rather than through fulfilling the Ten Commandments, as it were. Does Abram's moral lapse threaten to derail you from using him as a pillar of faith? Remember that God found him righteous because he believed, not because he lived life according to our sense of morality. His obedience was a natural result of his belief. My father would have commented that God expected Abram to walk in the light *he* had, not the light *we* have. What is the light we have, and how should we be walking in it? That said, I would be hard-pressed even to whisper a word of criticism, much less condemnation toward Abram for his lapse.

Membership Focus: *When you genuinely believe, you don't need motivational speakers. You don't need a dynamic orator to shame you into moving out on your belief (unless you just have low self-esteem).*

Key Insights for Prayer:

1. Pray that we can distinguish between beneficial customs and seemingly innocuous practices that contribute nothing at best and are detrimental at worse.

2. Pray that we would understand the difference between righteousness through obedience and righteousness through fulfilling the Ten Commandments, enabling us to step out in obedience, leaving the other to the Holy Spirit.

Acting Out – In closing this discussion, let me draw attention to one other consequence of believing. Odd way of expressing it, but you'll see what I mean. An Associate Pastor of a church I formerly attended asked the Wednesday night prayer group, "Do we act on what we believe?" Older seasoned Christians in the group immediately shot back, "No!" Their perspective was that the flesh is weak so, we sometimes act contrary to what we believe. The Associate Pastor replies, "Yes, we do act on what we believe." His perspective was that we sometimes speak contrary to what we truly believe – our actions betray our beliefs.

That exposes two truths. First, belief drives obedience, and the expression of our obedience signifies our beliefs. Second, we have a propensity to deceive ourselves on what we genuinely believe. If anyone says they embrace their church's vision but don't act on it for a legitimate reason, do they honestly believe it? Everything that transpired after Abram said "Ok" was the logical outcome of saying "Ok." Cause and effect.

Membership Focus: *Regarding God's calling on your church, aren't you just called to believe?*

Believe the Impossible

Only One Thing God Asks of You Revisited – I want to revisit the idea of God's expectation of Abram and Sarai and His expectation of us by extension. Have you ever wondered why God waited until after the fiasco with Hagar before telling Abram, "Oh! By the way, Sarai will have your son"? I thought that too. I wish I could give a profound answer as to why, but I don't have one. However, what it does for us is reinforce the understanding that God didn't expect Abram to understand the impossible. And in this capacity, He did not expect Abram to act as though he understood the impossible. God did not expect Abram to believe in something of which he had no comprehension. As alluded to earlier, when in Haran, God didn't tell Abram the details of who the mother would be, so Abram and Sarai had nothing to go on regarding what to believe – possible or impossible. Hence, Abram didn't know to place his faith in the impossible until God told him what that impossible was. Insofar as meeting God's expectations, Abram was expected to believe the impossible once God informed him. Was that too much to ask of Abram? Is it too much to ask of us?

Membership Focus: *Do you believe that the God who can do the impossible* **will** *do the impossible? We run a danger of becoming jaded to believing the unbelievable, and this is how. When we set the bar for God, and He doesn't clear it, our capacity is compromised. So, when God is the one who sets the bar, our ability to believe is weakened. We don't set the bar; He does.*

Is the Impossible Necessary – So, let's focus for a moment on whether the miracle that God bestows on your church is as dramatic as the ones we read in the Bible. At the same time, we will address the one He does confer on you. The answer to both issues is the same – **is a miracle necessary** to achieve God's objective? God has never performed miracles to impress people; He performed miracles to get their attention. Now it may have had the effect of impressing them, but that's not why He did them. I equate the latter with eliciting the desired response and the former with entertainment.

Membership Focus: *If your ministry initiative is successful beyond your expectations, that should elicit a humble response simply because that is compelling evidence that God is among you. It's also clear evidence that God performed a miracle to achieve His intended purpose in your church. The moral of the story is to trust God and believe Him for the impossible – even if it is impossible.*

By extension, there is one additional application for the Church. Fundamentally, it should strike a note of appreciation and realization that we, as Christians, are children of God as much as Abraham and Sarah were. However, we need to understand that Abraham's descendants, the Jewish people, enjoy a special relationship with God. They are His chosen people, but we are his adopted people. Prayer-wise, in this capacity, we should all strive to have faith like Abraham. What are some seemingly impossible things that God would have you believe for your church family?

Membership Focus: *A word of caution. Make sure the impossible is something God calls you and your church to do. There is a real danger of conjuring up something and expecting God to honor it just because you think you are supposed to have tremendous faith. Faith is an attribute instilled by God to do His work, not an instrument of manipulation to make God honor our work.*

Let's pause for a prayer pointer.

Key Insight for Prayer: Pray for the discernment to distinguish between legitimate faith that steps up to God's impossible and blind faith that leaps into mission impossible not ordained of God.

Quantity or Quality – Because we design ministries to serve various target groups, we tend to measure our ministries' success by church growth. In one sense using church growth as a measure of success is reasonable. Understood correctly it's safe to include church growth in the concept of reproduction? Consider your church numbers. Are you growing, or do you remain stagnant? We touched on this above about managing the status quo.

Don't be falsely pacified into thinking that numbers don't matter. To be sure, in certain respects, numbers don't matter, chiefly if it's a point of pride like David's act of taking a census in Israel (2nd Samuel). Also, numbers shouldn't be a central focus if you are a small congregation, as long as you are growing. In other words, don't look at the membership of the First Church of Metropolis and wonder what you are doing wrong because you aren't as big as they. That is another application of the Master-Slave Principle. Numbers matter in the sense that numerical growth should be a natural consequence of spiritual growth. In that context, numbers are the slave to spiritual growth. When numerical growth becomes the focus, that is when we wrongly use them. In that context, we elevate numbers to the level of master. Membership then ceases to be the measure of spiritual growth and becomes the central focus.

The aspect of numbers being a point of pride, however, can go both directions. If you know of a nearby congregation that is not growing, are they making it a point of pride or self-accomplishment? "Well, we don't have quantity, but we have quality." It does matter, and it may very well be an act of denial in that congregation.

Every legitimate church is God's agent in the world. So growth should be a natural byproduct of a church's impact on the community. If that is not apparent, God may not be active in that church. And if God isn't engaged in that church, why isn't He. It's not because of physical limitations. It may be because of spiritual stagnation. He can't do any miracles when unbelief or being lukewarm (same as unbelief) abound. A lack of faith and unbelief will prevent the Holy Spirit from divinely intervening in our lives with a miracle from above. Read Matt 13:58. That passage of scripture indicates that the Savior cannot and will not do many marvelous works for the unbelieving heart. In closing out this thought, numbers should be an indicator parameter, not a target goal or a basis for boasting.

Life Event Number 3 - Abraham

Impossible to Believe?

Having Not Apprehended – The expression of unbelief in a church is that of walking by sight. Once it takes hold, it's like Cuban Jute; it's almost impossible to root it out.

I want to introduce a prayer pointer that goes hand in hand with a prayer pointer in Adam and Eve: Walking by faith and not by sight.

Key Insight for Prayer: Pray that God will uproot any spirit of unbelief from your church. Pray that the leadership will be willing to take on the risk of leading the charge to walk by faith.

The aspect of walking by sight may not always be due to obstinate unbelief. It could be as simple as unrealized faith. Here is what I mean by that. Many of us, and maybe all of us, tend to live in a fantasy world where our dreams and aspirations are high profile and 100% successful. And, of course, we are the hero in our fantasies. We don't step out to pursue the realization of our dreams because of a fear of failure. That is why we spend all our time in our fantasy world because we are never failures in our fantasy world. Plainly stated, this is an opiate, a form of bondage.

Here is our prayer pointer for this type of bondage.

Key Insight for Prayer: Pray that laity and leadership alike would step out of their fantasy world and into the reality of pursuing God's calling and purpose for your church.

The Proof is in the Pudding – By now, we all should be on the same page and aspiring to develop our faith. But we may be curious about how genuine and active our personal faith is. Are our prayers effective as a result? Or should it be rephrased that the effectiveness of our prayers reflects the depth of our faith? Here's one litmus test. True faith always focuses on the supernatural and not necessarily on the natural. We typically express counterfeit faith by setting the bar at what is humanly possible. When God works a miracle that defies common sense, the faithless explain it by natural phenomena, which could mean two things. It could mean the skeptics aren't true believers. More than likely, it means they have never exercised their faith. Perhaps they have never been in a situation that forced them to trust God. When we are in the habit of not exercising faith, it is difficult for us to believe that an act of God is indeed an act of God and not some fluke of nature.

Membership Focus: *God-inspired and directed faith will let you know when to step out of the natural and into the supernatural to achieve phenomenal results. What am I saying here? I am drawing a distinction between blind faith and Hebrews 11:1 faith. Step out in faith only if your spirit bears witness with God's spirit to do so. Then believe God for it, beloved. I'll be honest, the first time you or your church does this, it is scary.*

Life Event Number 3 - Abraham

My pastor's experience illustrates this point perfectly. The group of devoted Cypress pioneers I spoke of earlier was from our church. They were part and parcel of his vision. It would have been quite natural for him not to act on his dream. He could have said, "I must be mistaken." He could have decided he couldn't coordinate all the talented, astute, and intelligent church members who are business owners and executives in their everyday lives. When he was getting blowback from the naysayers (who, by the way, were business owners and executives), he could have said, "They know better than I do." When the funds were not there to give him the green light, he could have given up. When the finances were nothing more than the "substance of things hoped for," he could have joined the ranks of those who walked away from God's call. He could have then witnessed others step up to take the reward. In short, he could have done what came naturally to him. Thank God he didn't choose that alternative.

Instead, he kept his eyes on the Lord and visualized life from a supernatural point of view. Praise God! As of this book's writing, the new campus has been in service for about nine years. Since its inception, this campus has been responsible for ushering more than 600 souls into the kingdom. The current average attendance is more than 1200 adults each Sunday. That is in a community with a population of roughly 82,000. They also have an excellent discipleship ministry. The fruit all this has yielded is that they are now an independent, stand-alone church.

The Dough is Still Rising – It's wise to ask for wisdom and discernment on when to step out of the natural. We shouldn't need any reminder to keep our gaze affixed on the Savior at all times. Contrary to what I said before, sometimes we must be satisfied with the status quo until He gives us a directive to do otherwise. So, if it sounds like I vacillate between saying "Go," "Don't Go," it's because I'm trying to walk that fine line between knowing when to go and knowing when to stand still. We have a propensity to go when God says stand still and stand still when God says Go. We may need to stand still if God is at work preparing hearts. He can also be busy maturing His saints in their walk. An extra measure of maturational development may need to take place for the task that lies ahead. Along these lines, I recall a sermon I once heard on the Exodus. The preacher noted that the Israelites suffered greatly in the days leading up to the Exodus to strengthen them for the journey ahead. When God is ready, He can work in surrendered hearts and wills. He will transform the natural into a remarkable supernatural ministry or event for His glory.

<u>Key Insight for Prayer:</u> Pray that you and your church members will be prepared perfectly for the dynamics He desires to put into play for your church body.

Membership Focus: *Remember this: Faith is your ticket to the miraculous. So, ask yourself: since I'm beginning a brand-new venture, why wouldn't I want to start it off with a miracle. Believe God expectantly. Your's may not happen tomorrow or maybe not even next year, but I promise you it will happen in God's time.*

How do I know this? Simple, the Word guarantees it.

Guideline Wrap Up: Faith & Obedience or Obedience & Faith?

If the scripture is accurate from beginning to end in how God revealed His grand plan to Abraham, it was step by step from small to grandiose over an extended period. As someone has once wisely said, "God's never in a hurry, but He's never late."

Also, keep in mind that Abraham never saw his great nation come to pass in his lifetime. All he saw were his grandchildren: Jacob and Esau, which were about 15 years old when Abraham died. However, he was not without compensation for his obedience to God. By the time Sarah passed on, Abraham was already very wealthy, as noted in his negotiations with the Hittites to purchase a burial place. And before that, there is also the incident where he rescued Lot from Chedorlaomer and his allies. Abraham was a pretty formidable force to be reckoned with then. So, God blessed him in this regard, but Abraham was never a king of any nation.

Membership Focus: *If God calls your church to such glorious heights, are you willing to be satisfied with the prospect of not seeing your "great nation."*

The wisdom of acquiring an attitude of faith will yield one other fabulous result: the ability to please God. The book of Hebrews states that without faith, it is impossible to do just that. The Bible heroes in the book of Genesis set examples of how this can materialize in the lives of God's saints. How thrilling! What a noble thing to do! How humbling! We can bring joy and delight to our Lord and Creator's heart.

But there is one other necessary element. If I may borrow from James, *"Faith without works is dead."* Beginning and ending in obedience is a wise thing to do for the follower of God. As noted in the opening paragraphs to Abraham, obedience and faith are inextricably bound up together. Obeying God's Word and His daily directives enables us to be at the right place, with the right person at the right time.

I derived the following prayer pointer from subplots in Abraham's life.

Key Insight for Prayer: Pray that your church will not be detoured, derailed, or discouraged from its ordained endpoint by all the challenges that arise on the way.

Guideline #7: Begin with Proper Planning: Timing is Everything.

Applicability

- **Target Population:** Church Leadership

Genesis 18:14: *Is anything too hard for the LORD? At the appointed time I will return to you, according to the time of life, and Sarah shall have a son.*

Topical Delineation and Elaboration

Our Counsel Not Required

Regarding Abraham's life, this guideline addresses the affliction of tunnel vision. He was so focused on his perceived path he couldn't see what was going on in his peripheral vision. Because of that, he attempted to compensate for it by force-fitting the goal he saw in his tunnel vision. This analogy demonstrates how Abram's and Sarai's circumstances blinded them from seeing God's ability to circumvent those circumstances. From the moment they left Haran until the Lord announced Isaac's arrival, the conflict between God's promise and Sarah's barrenness probably played constantly on both their minds. God's timing was not Abram's timing. No amount of consternation, wheedling, begging, threatening, manipulating, or even providing well-thought-out and objective arguments on

Abram's part would move God from His appointed date. God did not seek Abram's partnership or counsel in this decision. Let's not complicate the issue by theorizing that there could have been some action on Abram's part that may have influenced God's timetable.

We've probably all heard or proclaimed this at one time or another, "Boy, that sure was God's timing." We typically say it in context with time-critical issues about which we have been praying. But does it have any significance beyond its face value; what do we mean when we speak of it? Does it mean that God finally caved in like the unjust judge (Lk 18:1-5) and answered our prayer in the nick of time? Or does it mean He wanted to see how badly we wanted it? I don't know that anyone can answer that question. I suspect there are situations where persistence has zero influence on God's appointed time. And no amount of praying will change that. For those situations in which we are encouraged to be persistent, how does He answer? Does he answer based on our persistence, or does He answer based on His timing – or both? I don't know that we can answer these questions either. However, there are two things we can say with confidence:

1. Prayer is a definite factor in receiving an answer from God. It is enormously presumptuous on our part to assume that we will receive anything from God if we expect Him to care about it more than we do. Let me qualify that. When you take a child by the hand to lead them to their favorite ride at a theme park, you expect them to walk with you, not make you drag them along. When we take the stance that our inability to meet a need exempts us from cooperation or taking a vested interest in that need, we shouldn't expect God to provide.

2. Any issue that merits enough attention to pray about will probably have a window of opportunity assigned by God. To not pray or to delay in praying may result in missing that window.

Triage Prayer Ministries

One situation we don't want to work ourselves into is a triage prayer ministry. That's where we develop a cavalier attitude in praying for time-sensitive issues under the misconception that because they are not imminent, they are not immediately vital. That doesn't necessarily mean we ignore these issues. It means we rank them low priority to focus on issues perceived as critical. The net result is that they have become time-critical by the time we rerank them as a high priority. So, here is the appropriate cliché. Let's not make our lack of planning an emergency on God's part. The timing or the *"when"* in our prayers is essential. It is all part and parcel of getting direction from the Father, being obedient to the Holy Spirit, following His instructions, and tracking with His schedule, not ours. It means we will never get ahead of the Lord nor lag in terms of his will, plan, and purpose for our lives. Because we do not discover the ministry or establish the objectives and goals, neither do we set the schedule.

In a statement, whenever you begin any new ministry or Christian service in your church, staying close to God means being *synchronized* with His timetable at all times. In many respects, our role in this guideline is to wait, fervently praying while we wait. But when it's time to move out, it's time to move out. We will talk more about God's timetable in Exodus.

Key Insight for Prayer: Ask God to instill a sense of trust in His patterns, sequence of events, and timing in the leadership. May they grow according to His will and not skip any steps along the way.

Guideline #8 – Begin in Covenant with God

Applicability

- **Target Population:** Church Body at Large

Genesis: 18:14: *Is anything too hard for the LORD? At the **appointed time** I will return to you, according to the time of life, and Sarah shall have a son.*

Topical Delineation and Elaboration

Let's Covenant Together

The Fulcrum – For this Guideline, let's flashback to a time before Isaac was born, to a time when Abram and Sarai were still in the dark on their progeny. In the 15th chapter of Genesis, God waxes eloquent, telling Abram in a vision that He is his shield and exceedingly great reward. And then Abram spoils the moment by complaining about not having a child. He quickly follows this up with the comment that Eliezer, his house servant, will become his heir because of this. At this moment, God breaks the news that Abram will have an heir from his own body. He also takes him outside and tells him to look up and count the stars. When God says, "So shall your descendants be," Abram **believes**. That is the pivotal point in Abram's life when God ascribes his belief as righteousness.

That was Part A of God's revelation to Abram and probably all he was interested in hearing. But God wasn't finished with the conversation. Proceeding with Part B, God then tells him, *"I am the Lord, who brought you out of Ur of the Chaldeans, to give you this land to inherit it."* Hearing that your offspring will be as the sand of the sea is pretty overwhelming. But learning that the land is also yours probably resulted in mental overload. Mustering as much diplomacy as he could, Abram essentially says, prove it. In the ensuing verses, God takes Abram through a covenant ceremony that follows a definite order. It calls for the sacrifice of a 3-year old heifer, a 3-year old female goat, a 3-year old ram, a turtle dove, and a young pigeon. Abram cuts the larger animals in half and places the halves opposite each other. The birds are left whole.

As the sun goes down, Abram goes into a deep sleep, receiving what appears to be the first prophecy with specificity regarding his descendants. God tells him the Jews will sojourn as slaves in Egypt for 400 years. That will end with their subsequent deliverance and return to Canaan. Now here is where we need to pay attention to the details of the ceremony. After the sun goes down, poof, a smoking firepot with a torch, appears and passes between the pieces. *On the same day the Lord made a covenant with Abram, saying: To your descendants I give this land, from the river of Egypt to the great river, the River Euphrates – the kenites, the kenizzites, the Kadmonites, the Hittites, the Perizzites, the Rephaim, the Amorites, the Canaanites, the Girgashites and the Jebusites* (Genesis 15: 18-21). So anytime you hear someone mention the Abrahamic Covenant, that is what we just summarized.

What it All Means – This covenant ceremony, including the various elements and sequence of events, was a standard practice of that day. According to Matthew Henry's Commentary, they used animals three years of age *"because then they were at their full growth and strength: God must be served with the best we have, for He is the best."* Biblical scholars would also say this ceremony is an example of Christ typology. Animals three years of age have achieved developmental perfection and, by application, represent Christ, who is the perfect sacrifice. The act of dividing the animals signifies sacrifice through death. And, of course, all this is also interpreted as a Type Christ in its symbology. Let's return to a discussion on how this passage's meaning can make the rubber meet the road in praying for your church.

When you read about a covenant in the bible, substitute the word "contract" in its place. That will give you a good idea of how it translates into our modern-day cultural equivalent. Two or more parties make a binding contract in which each party gives up something to get something in return. Ok, test question. What is missing in the agreement between God and Abram? If you answered that the entire burden of the contract appears to fall on God and that the benefits appear to be weighted heavily in favor of Abram, you answered correctly. So, what was Abram's obligation, if any, in this contract? Two, to be exact: to *believe* and to *persevere* in his journey. That plays into what we've already discussed: that the act of believing drove Abram to persevere. Like Noah, the mere act of obedience has little longevity without something to feed it. In Noah's case, I focus on his *invested sense of purpose.* In Abram's case, I focus on his *act of believing*, but if you said purpose and belief apply equally to Noah and Abram, you would be correct.

Membership Focus: *Do you trust in God to provide? Do you hold that the vision and purpose statements written and ratified by your church transcend the collective intelligence of your church body? Finally, do you genuinely accept the belief that God Himself* *appointed your church's vision and purpose? If you do, if you see your vision and purpose statement as more than mere rhetoric and more than just a paper god, then do the following. Bind together in agreement with God. Bind together with God on what dream to strive for in your church and pray toward that end. Abram's only obligation was to believe and put one foot in front of the other. In our case, our only role is to believe and put one foot in front of the other. But this kind of obedience is something that we must do by choice. As discussed above, receiving a calling isn't like an amusement park ride where the Holy Spirit drives, and we just sit back and enjoy the ride.*

So, what prayer pointers can we draw from this? By now, you are probably way ahead of me on identifying relevant prayer pointers. That said, don't limit yourself to the ones I present. Read between the lines and come up with some of your own.

Key Insight for Prayer: Pray that your church collectively binds together in agreement with God to accept your church's vision and purpose as ordained by Very God. Pray that they embrace that vision and purpose as being tailored specifically for your church by God Himself (Notice I did not say vision and purpose statement.)

Membership Focus: *Assemble your prayer team and bind together in agreement with God. Uplift His calling for your church, as well as the road that your church will take in getting there.*

What is Sacrifice? Really!

Throughout this discussion, two elements may have nagged at the back of your mind. You may have wondered why I didn't draw them out into guidelines. In the case of one element, it is an artificial force fit. To be fair, it has peppered the discussion throughout. That element is sacrifice. When Abraham went up Mt. Moriah to sacrifice Isaac, it wasn't his idea. He wasn't doing it to appear noble or humble or spiritual. He did it out of obedience. That is the undergirding principle justifying faith. When faith assists obedience, small beginnings blossom into magnanimous edifices. When faith synergizes obedience, there is satisfaction in sacrifice.

Sacrifice comes in two forms which we can boil down to one underlying motivator. The two states are *obedience* and *priorities*. Abraham sacrificed out of obedience – that was his priority. You and I sacrifice out of priorities – that is our obedience. Please don't take that as a clever literary device with a veiled compliment. It's not. We sacrifice to that which we hold dear –typically recreational pursuits. You thought I was going to say church, didn't you? We can consolidate the two forms of sacrifice into one principle: obedience to that we hold dear. We love to shop, so when the shopping mall calls, we obey. We love to play golf, so when the golf course calls, we mind. We love to fish, so when the fish are biting, we submit. So, when unreached suburbia cries for spiritual deliverance….

Abraham held dear his relationship with God. That drove his obedience.

Key Insight for Prayer: Pray that you and your fellow congregants would be able to differentiate between sacrificing out of priorities and sacrificing out of obedience.

You Know, the Other Element?

You're Not Going to Like This – So, sacrifice is one of two elements mentioned above. The other element is not something you can pursue, or at least no one in their right mind does. It's more a consequence than a pursuit. It's probably equally dangerous to pray for it, and at this point, you probably know to what I'm referring. That element is patience. Do you reckon that after waiting 25 years for Isaac to come along, Abram developed some patience? Typically, we acquire it because we have to, not because of the benefit it affords us. We avoid the process of acquiring patience because it is unpalatable. It is something life drags us into kicking and screaming. We develop it through trial.

> *And not only so, but we glory in tribulations also: knowing that tribulation worketh patience* (Romans 5:3, KJV)

But You May Be Called to Endure It – Life is replete with trials, all of which contribute to developing patience. Most of which we weather without harmful consequences. I want to step you through one such testing that is near and dear to me because I've been through it. It's likely that you, also, will experience the same test sometime in your spiritual walk, if you haven't already.

Here is how it plays out. For any number of reasons, your church has gotten into a slump. Church life is so routine and mechanical you waver between discouragement and frustration. Others are very much aware of the problem. And like you, they don't have the position or the authority to do anything about it. Those who can do something about it don't seem to be inclined to do so – at least, that's how it appears from your perspective. Alternatively, the leadership may be working hard to do something about it but to no avail because all their efforts are "gimmick-based programs." Stagnation has set in; stagnation with an odd sense of comfort about it – a sense of comfort that's more akin to lethargy than contentment. Members incrementally leave for greener pastures, resulting in a relentless and persistent downward spiral in church vitality.

Some lay leaders passionately believe the solution is to renovate and update the facilities. They consider it necessary to attract new congregants, actually thinking that attractive facilities are your church's only chance of redemption at this point. However, the decimation of the membership results in a corresponding decline in available funds for such renovations. In concert with the financial experts, the leadership prioritizes available funds: paid staff first, utilities next, and the remainder apportioned between building maintenance or existing ministries. The building maintenance team is resorting to putting band-aids on band-aids by this time. It devolves into a condition where the church's central focus is to keep its head above water. But at the same time, making it look like a sinking ship was never in question; thank you very much! It's a noble attempt at maintaining the status quo that's not status.

Sailing into the Sunset – You find yourself considering the unthinkable option of pursuing the greener pastures others have already gone after. You wrestle with the question of whether it's better to be a fool and stay onboard or be a traitor and pursue the greener pastures. You hear from recently departed church members telling you to quit beating a dead horse. Come over to their new church where Pastor F. Lawless is "just absolutely marvelous." The very thought of forsaking your church and shifting your share of the burden onto your fellow congregants wins the argument for the present. You justify it with the caveat that you can move later on if things get too bad.

You feel trapped and torn between riding it out or giving up, but to what are you surrendering? That's **your** church, the people **you** know and love, the place where **you** established your roots –

perhaps a little too well. That's the church where you have invested so much of your life, so giving up and going elsewhere is not an option, not yet, at least. Oh! And to add insult to injury, your pastor just "got called" to go someplace or do something, not sure which, but it doesn't matter; he's abandoned ship and can't help us now.

You have now entered uncharted waters. It begins with an unsettling realization that you're it – no reinforcements are coming to rescue you. There is no authority figure you can appeal to who will chart a course to get us out of this mess. It's just us now. Oddly enough, church business continues as usual. The deacons and elders are now in charge. However, they are not going to make any significant decisions regarding the church's direction. That will be the new pastor's job – whenever he arrives. Their job is to maintain course until he does get there. So, the church is on autopilot, which is status quo without a destination.

A search committee is appointed, and hopes are high that a "qualified" candidate will answer the call quickly – the same "qualified" candidate described in Adam and Eve. Weeks turn into months and months to years. Everyone is coping through positive encouragements to one another, yet with a guarded disposition bordering on gloom. In the meantime, you are relying on interim pastors, some which you would love to take on permanently. But church policy forbids that due to conflicts of interest with the interim pastor's day job or ministry. Hope fades into acceptance and acceptance into discouragement.

That resolve to conquer, to take the bull by the horns that you felt at the beginning, begins to sputter like an engine low on fuel. You eventually realize that you don't have any control over the outcome of events and never did. Don't whitewash it; this trial you are experiencing is a form of tribulation. It's not life-threatening.

Life Event Number 3 - Abraham

You're not going to lose your job (unless perhaps you are on staff), and no one is persecuting you for your faith. It's just an unsettling discomfort like floating downstream without oars or a tiller in a boat that is propelled purely by hope. You would like to think it's faith-driven, but at this point, you're not sure how functional that is.

Your opportunity to go to greener pastures has all but slipped away. After your wrestling match with yourself, more people have left, leaving more of a burden on you – you are now part of the remnant, the stalwart, the dedicated. All you can do is ride it out and hope for anything short of a crash landing. There is no relief on the horizon, but you remain hopeful that it can't last forever. In what faith you have left, you maintain that it won't end in disaster. It's now twilight at your church.

Relief at Last! – WOO HAH! A new pastor has answered the call. Declare it from the rooftop, broadcast it to the populous. He is now on board. He is passionate. He is energetic, and he is not letting any grass grow under his feet.

Life Event Number 3 - Abraham

Your church is in full swing with multiprong ministry initiatives and redirections using all of the new-fangled, updated ministry methodologies, and it's all hands on deck. Young families are joining in droves, and people are giddy with euphoric jubilation. It's lead, follow, or get out of the way. In many respects, you feel like you are flying by the seat of your pants and can't stop long enough to assess your progress or even catch your breath. Everything is a blur. You are so busy carrying out your own assigned tasks that you have no idea how the big picture looks, much less how your assignment fits into the big picture. You are not even sure there is a big picture.

But after a few months of this, the honeymoon is over. The new pastor is yanking everyone out of their comfort zone by leading the church in ways that "we've never done it that way before." He has even committed a couple of abominations, like moving the piano from one side of the stage to the other without proper authorization. He is entrusting assignments to people who feel unqualified for said assignments, and you agree. Frustration levels rise, tempers flare, and you begin to wonder, "what have we gotten ourselves into?" The tribulation pendulum has swung full-course. You bottomed out at the prospect of having to close the church doors. And then you pivoted to the opposite extreme. You now have the dilemma of how to shut the church doors at the end of the day. You can't say you've jumped from the frying pan into the fire because you weren't in the frying pan in the first place and whatever you jumped into is not exactly a fire. It's more like trying to stay ahead of a stampeding herd.

During the few respites you've availed yourself, you find yourself lapsing into a longing for the plumbing leaks and onions back in good ol' Egypt. Then you are shaken out of your stupor with the realization that the good ol' days weren't so good. The thought of going back to the routine drudgery provokes demoralizing memories. So, you forge on knowing that at least you are in motion. You don't know whether you are going forward or in circles, but you go.

What it All Means, Again – When the dust settles, you look around at those who chose not to participate. You wonder *what is wrong* with them that they constantly whine like babies about trivial issues. They continually criticize the staff for not meeting their juvenile wants. They sound kind of like the way you may have sounded before getting involved in this experience. They demonstrate no strength of character:

- strength of character that comes with enduring hardships,
- strength of character that comes with uncertainty and conflict,
- strength of character that comes with exhaustion and sacrifice.

Now I may have overdramatized the above scenario a little bit. But it answers the question of what trials and tribulations have to do with patience. Does it, however, answer the question of what the sacrifice has to do with patience? I'll let the Apostle Paul answer that question by finishing the thought he started.

> *And not only that, but we also glory in tribulations, knowing that tribulation produces perseverance; and perseverance, character; and character, hope.* (Romans 5:3-4- NKJV) (note I switched versions from KJV to NKJV).

So what does patience have to do with sacrifice? Without tribulation, there is no perseverance. Without perseverance, there is no sacrifice; hence the former is the vehicle for the latter. Perseverance and patience are two sides of the same coin. While the King's James essentially equates the two (KJV vs. NKJV), I differentiate between them. Patience is the strength to persevere, and perseverance builds patience. It is kind of like pulling yourself up by your bootstraps.

In the vicarious experience that I just walked us through with you as the central character, you put your spiritual growth on hold because of what you valued most. You sacrificed your time – time you cannot recover. You allowed time to slip away, the time you might have better used at that "marvelous" church. You did that all in the hopes of salvaging something you *invested* your life in, something you *believe* to be more precious – your church and the niche your God has appointed for your church. Then slowly but surely, you come to the full realization that the sacrifice of putting your spiritual growth on hold wasn't a sacrifice. It was an investment; it was part of your spiritual growth – something you can't learn in the pews or small group Bible study. Did you ask for it? No. Did you seek it out? No. But without your permission, it sought you out.

Key Insight for Prayer: Pray that you and your fellow travelers will be resolute in weathering protracted trials so that you may reap the maximum benefit in patience.

Guideline Wrap Up: Tying It Up with a Bow

Four Things – There we have it. That gives us four things for which to pray. They are obedience, faith, patience, and sacrificial giving. All four variables have a reciprocal relationship to the materialization of the vision God has placed in your hearts. How is this so? Again, "*Early [and original] sparks of faith will serve as an example of how you can increase your faith for things on down the road.*" (bracketed text added)

Membership Focus: *Let me take a page from Peter's playbook (with some modifications). Beloved, do not think it strange concerning unscheduled crises which try you, as though something that wasn't supposed to happen to you has happened. Don't assume that God is so distracted with more important things that the crisis you are now experiencing somehow slipped past Him without notice.*

I learned long ago that if I'm going to suffer under a trial, I want the full benefit of that trial, and that is the end to which I pray. And beloved, that is the end to which I encourage you to pray as well.

Throughout our discussion of Abraham, we have let obedience serve as an undercurrent. Let's close by enumerating how obedience and faith factor into small beginnings. Following is an expanded summary of the quote, "*Early sparks of faith will serve as our example of how you can increase your faith for things on down the road.*"

Obedience

1. Obedience requires a Game Plan: that implies a beginning (that doesn't mean we know what the game plan is).
2. Obedience plays out one step at a time
3. Obedience is not always popular (Noah).

4. Obedience does not always feel good (waiting 25 years for something you thought should have happened 24 years earlier).

Faith

5. Faith is the precursor to obedience
6. Faith requires complete obedience, not partial obedience (you don't test the waters to see if you want to commit fully or not).
7. By definition, faith requires obedience divorced from our ability (it does not come naturally).
8. Faith defies human reasoning and common sense.

As stated above, obedience, faith, patience, and sacrifice have a reciprocal relationship. Here it is:

- Faith drives obedience, and obedience feeds faith.
- Faith advances patience, and patience sustains faith.
- Finally, faith fosters sacrifice, and sacrifice strengthens faith.

That brings our treatment of Abraham to a close. Following is our summary list of prayer pointers, after which we will move onto Jacob.

Summary List of Prayer Pointers from Abraham

➤ Pray that the saints in your church body would embrace this growth model from infancy to maturity as being ordained by God irrespective of their maturity level.

➤ Pray that understanding the growth process would encourage and not discourage someone's decision to submit to discipleship, start a new ministry, or even launch a new church.

➤ Intercede for your church's leadership and all its ministry participants to not become overly ambitious and attempt to run faster than God wants you to run. Your church leadership's near-term goals should start at the pilot program level and build from there. It's not about God's limitations but our limitations. Rest assured, your ministry will become God-size when He feels you have grown to that point.

➤ Pray that immature saints in your church body would not avoid discipleship out of fear that they will have to forfeit their comfort zone.

➤ Pray that all who have chosen to start a new ministry or submit to discipleship understand that testings and dry periods are part of the growth process. These, too, are ordained of God to produce character.

➤ Ask for a sense of ownership over your church's beginnings, current status, and future destiny.

➤ Pray for discernment of what is sacred and what is not. Holding the wrong things as sacred can derail you from advancing to greater heights.

- Pray that God would instill an attitude of sacrifice in the hearts of your church members.
- Pray for vision and innovative ideas on implementing these visions in a manner compatible with God's master plan.
- Pray that your church develops a sensitivity to God's leading to choose what stimulates growth. Pray that no failure would be in vain, but God would bring victory out of disappointment.
- Pray that the laity would forge ahead even in the face of drudgery and monotony.
- Pray that fellow saints will not falter at the task's enormity but be encouraged by the distance they have already come.
- Pray that we can distinguish between beneficial customs and seemingly innocuous practices that contribute nothing at best and are detrimental at worse.
- Pray that we would understand the difference between righteousness through obedience and righteousness through fulfilling the Ten Commandments, enabling us to step out in obedience, leaving the other to the Holy Spirit.
- Pray for the discernment to distinguish between legitimate faith that steps up to God's impossible and blind faith that leaps into mission impossible not ordained of God.
- Pray that God will uproot any spirit of unbelief from your church. Pray that the leadership will be willing to take on the risk of leading the charge to walk by faith.
- Pray that laity and leadership alike would step out of their fantasy world and into the reality of pursuing God's calling and purpose for your church.

Life Event Number 3 - Abraham

- Pray that you and your church members will be prepared perfectly for the dynamics He desires to put into play for your church body.

- Pray that your church will not be detoured, derailed, or discouraged from its ordained endpoint by all the challenges that arise on the way.

- Ask God to instill a sense of trust in His patterns, sequence of events, and timing in the leadership.

- Pray that your church collectively binds together in agreement with God to accept your church's vision and purpose as ordained by Very God. Pray that they embrace that vision and purpose as being tailored specifically for your church by God Himself.

- Pray that you and your fellow congregants would be able to differentiate between sacrificing out of priorities and sacrificing out of obedience.

- Pray that you and your fellow travelers will be resolute in weathering protracted trials so that you may reap the maximum benefit in patience.

Life Event Number 3 - Abraham

Life Event Number 4 – Jacob

Jacob. All I can say is he was one piece of work. You are probably questioning my sanity at this choice. Why in the world would I choose a con artist like Jacob to represent any principles of prayer, except perhaps what not to do. I included Jacob because he appears to be the only one with the following two qualifying experiences.

1. He saw angels ascending and descending a ladder to heaven, and
2. He wrestled with God. And prevailed!

Let's treat these individually. I will tackle the first by coming in through the back door. So, it won't be immediately apparent what angels on a ladder have to do with the topic of the following guideline.

Guideline #9: Begin with A Prayer of Release from Our Past

Applicability

- **Target Population:** Individual Members

Jeremiah 31: 29: *In those days they shall say no more: "The fathers have eaten sour grapes, and the children's teeth are set on edge."*

Topical Delineation and Elaboration

Family Systems

I wonder if Isaac and Rebekah ever regretted naming him Jacob. In some cultures, words have power. The act of calling their son Supplanter could have been perceived as why he turned out to be a one. We can't possibly know what they were thinking, but I'm pretty sure that's not why he became a supplanter. Let me lay out the dynamics of how it all played out. When I was attending Texas Woman's University (TWU) for my family counseling degree, I took a course called "Family Systems." The fundamental premise is that certain personality traits, for good or bad, characterize the extended family down through the ages. For example, some families show a propensity toward substance abuse from one generation to the next. Other families show tendencies towards criminal behavior down through the family line. At the opposite end of the spectrum, some families are replete with pastors and ministers.

Jacob's family system showed a tendency toward deception and subversion from his mother's side. Grasping Esau's heel at birth may have been prophetic on God's part, but that's not what triggered it. Jacob didn't become a supplanter because he grabbed Esau's heel. His mother, Rebekah, taught him. Remember the goatskin trick (Genesis 27)? She was already a seasoned veteran, and so was Laban, Rebekah's brother and Jacob's uncle. It's entirely possible that Bethuel, Rebekah's and Laban's father, was also a con man. Where else would they have learned it? So, when Jacob landed at Uncle Laban's doorstep, he was fixin' to be schooled by the master. He played Jacob like a fiddle from the moment he arrived. First, Laban gave him Leah instead of Rachel and then convinced him to stick around for another seven years before giving him Rachel. To cap it all off, he did a lot of creative accounting with Jacob's wages.

Jacob quite probably would have walked away empty-handed had God not stepped in to officiate the sheep and goat wrangling competition. So you see, we really can't hold prenatal Jacob solely accountable for something passed on to him through his family line.

A Peek Behind the Curtain

But we are getting ahead of ourselves. Let's review Jacob's journey to Uncle Laban and capture a defining incident that changed everything Jacob was. That event was a dream in which he saw heaven open up with angels ascending and descending a ladder. More importantly, the Lord was at the top of the ladder, giving Jacob the same message He gave Abram. Based on the scriptural account, Jacob's vision was a lot more vivid than any ordinary dream. So, when Jacob awoke, he was understandably rattled by the experience. That one defining experience caused Jacob to take an about-face from being a supplanter to committing his life to God, even to the extent of tithing. Can you think of anything more miraculous than that, a person characteristically on the take, now giving? We can only speculate on what this con artist thought of God before his trip started. But the vision dispelled any doubt in Jacob's mind about the reality of God. I'm sure he quickly realized that the religious customs and rituals practiced by his forefathers were more than just going through the motions to appease a figment of their imagination. Before Jacob left home, Issac probably indoctrinated him about God, but that was all secondhand information. Now he had firsthand knowledge that there indeed was a spirit world out there, and he saw it with his own eyes.

Jacob's experience is one of those situations in which God breaks protocol by giving someone a peek behind the curtains the rest of us don't get to see. But who's complaining. Anytime God breaks protocol, it somehow works out to our advantage. For example, Saul's Damascus road experience resulted in God sending him to the Gentiles as an apostle (Gentiles are any of us who are not Jewish).

A note of caution on these types of revelations, once you receive it, you can't unsee it, and you are now accountable for what God expects of you as a result. That hearkens back to my comment that God only does miracles for achieving intended outcomes. He doesn't do them to entertain us (do it again, Daddy, do it again).

Fear or New Sight?

Resuming our discussion, we can surmise that this experience had the effect of **wowing** Jacob into reversing course on his life. It's more likely, however, that his response was due to having his spiritual blinders taken off. That is a phenomenon that also happened with Paul and possibly Abram.

Here is my interpretation of how it played out. Jacob probably became a con artist because that is what Rebeka modeled before him his whole life. It is what he thought was normal. It became second nature to him. For example, pathological liars don't necessarily have a conscious reason to lie; they just do. It's a defense mechanism for self-preservation or protection, i.e., the truth, any truth, can be held against them, so they lie.

Similarly, Jacob's subconscious (or maybe even conscious) motivation for being a con artist may have been self-preservation with the express purpose of not being at anyone's mercy! When

Jacob had his vision and realized God is real and will look out for him, he could drop the act. At that point, Jacob was no longer a prisoner of his past. He could walk away!

One other characteristic that may have helped Jacob cross over was a trait the Apostle Paul shared. In the integrity of their hearts, both Jacob and Paul did what they thought was correct or necessary. Before his conversion, Paul *knew* he was defending his God. After his conversion, he *knew* he was defending his God - the difference being how he viewed or understood God. Nothing in his's zeal for God had changed, only how Paul directed it. In Jacob's case, he had a radical change of heart, indicating he was not a pathological con artist but a con artist out of necessity. As a side note, anytime Bethel is mentioned in any Biblical accounts, Jacob's experience was how it got its name. Beth El, house of God.

Membership Focus: *You may have a less than favorable personal history or family history from which God has liberated you. However, going forward, you feel that you remain a prisoner of your past in some respects. You sense a low ceiling on your serviceability because church leadership hasn't entirely accepted you. Nothing has been said or implied, but it's just how ministry opportunities flow around you but don't entrain you.*

Key Insight for Prayer: Pray that God will fully release you from lingering relics of your past. Pray for the dissolution of barriers and perceptions that keep you a prisoner of your past.

Meanwhile, Back at Laban's Ranch

Resuming where we left off, Uncle Laban tried every maneuver he could to keep Jacob disadvantaged. As noted above, Jacob probably would have left empty-handed had God not stepped in. So, why did God rescue Jacob? It could be that He knew Laban had an unfair advantage, and He thought it was unseemly for a family member to cheat his nephew. That's a factor, but not the primary reason. God delivered Jacob because he was now God's chosen vessel. When God called Jacob at Bethel, Jacob responded in the affirmative. That one act altered the dynamics of Jacob's life from one of being his own advocate (as supplanter) to one in which God was his advocate. God didn't rescue Jacob because he was poor defenseless Jacob; he rescued him because he was His chosen vessel. And Laban was interfering with that chosen vessel. To Jacob, Laban's deceit was a mobile blockade. When Jacob stepped left, so did Laban; when Jacob stepped right, Laban followed suit. To God, Laban's shenanigans were only an annoying nuisance. Think back to our discussion on obstacles and paper tigers - overwhelming to us but minor irritants to God.

Membership Focus: *When your church body responds in the affirmative to God's calling, He will straighten your road. He will remove obstacles that obstruct and distract you from the destination God has set for you.*

Key Insight for Prayer: Pray that God will enable your leadership to see beyond obstacles the enemy throws in the road to block you from fulfilling God's calling.

So, this brings us to our second prayer guideline under Jacob. No, it's not that you would get a peek behind the curtains. I'm not sure I would ask for that unless you are willing to take on an elevated level of responsibility for what you see.

Guideline #10: Begin with A Prayer of Dedication

Applicability

- **Target Populations:** This has multilevel applicability
    1. Your church body as an entity
    2. Any ministry spawned by your church body, and
    3. The rank and file church member

Genesis 15:18: *On the same day the LORD made a covenant with Abram, saying: "To your descendants I have given this land, from the river of Egypt to the great river, the River Euphrates ....*

Genesis 28:13: *I am the Lord God of Abraham your father and the God of Isaac; the land on which you lie I will give to you and your descendants. Also your descendants shall be as the dust of the earth; you shall spread abroad to the west and the east, to the north and the south; and in you and in your seed all the families of the earth shall be blessed. Behold, I am with you and will keep you wherever you go, and will bring you back to this land; for I will not leave you until I have done what I have spoken to you.*

Deuteronomy 5:3: *The LORD did not make this covenant with our fathers, but with us, those who are here today, all of us who are alive.*

Deuteronomy 7:9: *Therefore, know that the LORD your God, He is God, the faithful God who keeps covenant and mercy for a thousand generations with those who love Him and keep His commandments;*

Deuteronomy 29:9: *Therefore, keep the words of this covenant, and do them, that you may prosper in all that you do.*

Topical Delineation and Elaboration

In the last guideline, we introduced the aspect of commitment in context with Jabob's turnabout. In this guideline, we will expand on that idea.

Between the Bookends

When people get a peek behind the curtains as Jacob did, what do they usually do? They wholly (in whole) dedicate themselves to God, not out of fear but out of a heightened understanding and an enhanced realization of the unseen spiritual realm. Park that in the back of your mind, and we'll come back to it. Now I want to bring in Jacob's second qualifying experience - his wrestling match with God. I will treat it as a complement to the first experience.

The Bible is somewhat scanty in the details leading up to the event. It reads like part of the story was left out. All we know is that Jacob splits his family up and sends them ahead in an attempt to keep Esau from killing them all. It wasn't that he was hiding behind them as a shield. He was using them as gift couriers to appease Esau before meeting him face to face. So, Jacob is left alone, and the next thing we know, a man is wrestling with him. There is no mention of who he is, where he came from, when he arrived, and not so much as a salutation. I think he was related to Melchizedek with no beginning and no end.

The noteworthy point is that Jacob wouldn't give up, even when the angel cried Uncle. So, it begs the question, at what point did Jacob know he was wrestling with God? If at the start, would he have engaged in the wrestling match or immediately acquiesced? After the wrestling match, the man says, *"Your name shall no longer be called Jacob, but Israel; for you have struggled with God and with men, and have prevailed."* How Incredible! *You have struggled with God and prevailed!* Whether Jacob persisted out of a survival instinct or obstinant pride, this event signifies Jacob's **tenacity**.

Now, let's bring the two incidents together. This event and the vision at Bethel are like bookends; they bracket Jacob's stay in Padan Aram. As far as I know, God didn't do a lot of revelating when Jacob was with Laban. He gives Jacob his first major revelation while going to Padan Aram and his second major revelation on his way back from Padan Aram. There are only two minor appearances while he is under Laban's roof, and those are when God tells Jacob to go home. Welcome to Padan Aram; now go home.

I believe there is significance in having these two momentous events bracket his stay in Padan Aram. There has to be a connecting thread. Is it reading too much into the narrative to say the first event was to secure Jacob's dedication and the second to test his devotion? I'll answer that later, but first, let's see what parallels there are with us? Touching on the first, none of us have had a peek behind the curtains as vivid as Jacob's, so we can't hitch our faith and our dedication to a vivid dream. Still, any born-again believer who has declared their allegiance to Christ has that base covered. Unlike Jacob, we have the complete story before us from beginning to end in the Bible – even the parts that haven't happened yet. Jacob didn't have that. We learn the outcome from the Bible, so we don't have to worry about devoting our ministry in vain. Jacob knew none of that. The scope of his comprehension was very narrow compared to ours. That should be sufficient motivation to elicit a willful response - to prayerfully devote your church or any new ministry wholly from the moment of its conception.

Life Event Number 4 - Jacob

Regarding the second event, do we wrestle with God? Commitment is relatively easy – once we get past ego. Conceptually speaking, it's an intuitive act with a predictable outcome. "God, I can't do this myself so, I commit this ministry to you." And it's done. To struggle with God, on the other hand, is somewhat vague and unpredictable. Just the thought of it is fraught with uncertainty and anxiety; otherwise, it wouldn't be a struggle? The inherent fear is the idea of losing. Having read the account of Jacob wrestling with God untold times during my lifetime, it has never struck me as relevant to modern-day Christendom until now. In the first place, why is it even a question for Christians? Under what conditions would we even expect a born-again believer to have to wrestle with God? I understand the struggle unbelievers endure as God draws them to Himself. But as a believer, what could I possibly hope to accomplish when wrestling with God?

Let's try and answer that question as we resume our analysis of Jacob. The significance of his wrestling match is that he prevailed. How so? I believe Matthew Henry best expressed that thought in his commentary, "*What was the success of the engagement?*" Or, as I would put it, what was the victory? He answers the question by stating, "*It was not in his own strength that he wrestled, nor by his own strength that he prevailed, but in and by strength derived from Heaven.*" He then follows that up with, "*We cannot prevail with God but in his own strength. It is his Spirit that intercedes in us, and helps out infirmities...*" In other words, the Spirit of God empowers us to be the victor. But the victor of what? Applying that concept to our churches, what is our success in struggling with God? What would you like for it to be? That the path to our goal would be straight and clear? That may be a benefit, but that's not the victory.

We don't understand what it means to wrestle with God because it is a foreign concept. I think we avoid it out of fear of committing a sacrilege or blasphemy? But there is a difference between wrestling with God and being adversarial with God. What does it mean to struggle with God? I don't completely comprehend it, but I'm sure it doesn't mean being antagonistic toward Him. I do think He wants us to wrestle with Him. I believe there is a dimension to devotion that compels us to wrestle with God. It's a way of reconciling spiritual conflicts in our lives. If these conflicts stay buried, does that not compromise our commitment or dedication?

Membership Focus: *Do not fear wrestling with God. Welcome it as a face-to-face encounter with God in which He strengthens your faith, love, commitment, and dedication. Receive it as an affirmation that God is taking a personal interest in keeping you on the path He has set for you. Take it as confirmation that He is intent on sharpening your focus and avoiding distractions.*

Key Insight for Prayer: Pray that God would give you and your fellow congregants the freedom to wrestle with Him on issues with which you and your church struggles.

Now, don't confuse struggling with God with adversity and hardships that plague our ministries. Those are external factors that seek to derail us. Wrestling with God arises from internal factors that impede our progress – chiefly our ambition and fleshly nature. When we wrestle with God, it's for the express purpose of realigning our spirit with God's Spirit. I believe that was the victory Jacob knowingly or unknowingly walked away with when he wrestled with God - a spiritual realignment.

Before moving on, let's take the idea of wrestling with God a step further and graft it into a subplot that has served as an undercurrent throughout the book. I previously touched on the concept that being created in the image of God carries with it the qualities of faith and love. We come into this world equipped with both but in an infantile state. But because freedom of choice is the one element of control God has fully vested in us, we can only nurture faith and love by struggling with Him. That is particularly true since we still have our fleshly nature.

Further, because our sense of dedication and devotion are byproducts of faith and love, those too are strengthened through trial. Again, it's a spiritual realignment, something we will experience throughout this life. Now, let me revisit a statement I made a few paragraphs ago. *"Is it reading too much into the narrative to say the first event was to secure Jacob's dedication and the second to test his devotion?"* No, it's not too much to say. In reality, I fell short. The second event not only tried his commitment but strengthened it. Testings from God will always build the quality He is testing. But I'm not finished with devotion yet.

What is Devotion?

Let's go back and recapture another statement I made earlier about Jacob's persistence in the wrestling match. But I want to add to it. *"Whether Jacob persisted out of a survival instinct or obstinate pride, this event signifies Jacob's tenacity, commitment, and dedication."*

Let's expand further on the concepts of commitment and dedication and take it to its practical endpoint? Despite its intuitive connotation, I want to cast the act of dedicating our work to the Master in light of the meaning of the word itself. Webster's Dictionary defines "dedicate" as devoting oneself or something to a sacred purpose (1979). I find it interesting that Webster defines it in religious terms and not secular terms. Underscore the word <u>devote</u> here, dears. The significance of its meaning is how it requires us to become wholly involved in the sacred purpose. But we must be <u>willing</u> to fully devote ourselves and every aspect of our ministry to Him. Such surrender could potentially cost us every single material thing we own for the object of our devotion. This ties in nicely with our discussion of obedience, priorities, and sacrifice under Abraham. In actuality, Christians in our current culture very seldom have to give up all their material possessions for the sake of the gospel. But if called on, would you do so? Probably not. So, the question then becomes, what are we willing to give?

Membership Focus: *What does devotion mean to you? What percentage of everything are you willing to give. Try and envision that for a moment. How deep into your discretionary or even nondiscretionary spending are you prepared to cut for a sacred purpose. What is your cutoff point? What is enough?*

These are hard questions to answer, and they are undoubtedly vague. Or are they? We can quickly resolve the issue by redirecting our query to a target that doesn't lie. As a preface to the answer, understanding our depth of devotion shouldn't be a problem since we exercise it regularly. Find out where all your time and money go. That not only reflects the object of your devotion but the depth of your dedication as well. Remember the discussion on the shopping mall and the golf course? If, by contrast, the target of our commitment is a new church plant or new ministry, that is where we would want our material possessions to go.

The point I want to drive home is the same point I made under Abraham. Most people who support a cause sacrifice because they want to, not because they are required. The requisite is what it takes whether you want to or not. The "want to" subordinates the requirement. *"Want to"* becomes the master; *"the requirement"* becomes the slave. In other words, you are not going to fulfill the conditions required by the sacrifice if you don't want to. The act of willingly giving your resources to a cause is the tangible indicator that you are devoted. That's why God loves a cheerful giver. That is in perfect alignment with sacrificial prayer in the discussion on prayer vigils. Don't fall for the misconception that you can claim devotion without sacrifice. That would be like saying to your fiancée, "I love you, but I don't want to sacrifice my freedom for you." But that's what we do in the church. It goes back to my Associate Pastor saying that we indeed act on what we believe. On this basis, I doubt that any of us in modern-day America fully dedicate our lives to God. I reiterate D.L. Moody's statement, "The world has yet to see what God will do with a man fully consecrated to Him" (1872).

Counting the Costs

One thing should be clear, though. We are all called <u>not</u> to offer Christ resources that cost us <u>nothing</u> (II Sam 24:24). That idea follows in the same vein as James' argument that faith without works is dead. Devotion without sacrifice is a facade. In this regard, Jesus warned His disciples to count the cost before following Him. So, did Abram weigh the costs when God called him? Earlier I used that in jest as an excuse Abram might have used if he decided to walk away from God's call. Did Jacob count the costs when God called him? To be realistic, I'm sure both Abram and Jacob reckoned the costs. Here is how I think they did that. And this is how we should as well. Keep in mind the price tag is not limited to what it takes to carry out the mission. It also includes what you are losing or walking away from in carrying out that mission. Here is how we should count the costs. Line Item 1: The Most-High God, the creator of heaven and earth, is calling. Line Item 2: See Line Item 1.

Let me translate. God is doing the calling, and our fate is in the hands of a God for whom *nothing is too hard*. Is there anything in life that will adequately compensate us for *rejecting* God's calling? But God is generally not the problem; our resolve to follow through on God's calling is typically the problem. That said, don't go into any ministry with the attitude that if the going gets tough, you can go home and leave it to those hard-core church members who take matters like this a little too far.

So, in your accounting process, be sure and count the cost of adversity, then proceed with answering God's call. Let's rehearse now.

- Line Item 1: The Most-High God, the creator of heaven and earth, is calling.
- Line Item 2: There will be adversity
- Total: Engage

Dedicating your church to God can also result in another delightful blessing. King Solomon discovered one when he committed the first temple to God. The glory of God filled and permeated this marvelous structure to the point that the priests could not continue to minister and had to leave. Wow! When we fully dedicate ourselves, I can't help but wonder how God might manifest his glory in our midst and our places of worship.

Key Insights for Prayer:

1. Pray that God will give you and your church the capacity to be fully devoted and willing to commit all of your material possessions if called upon to do so. (Is it not in God's ability to replace those possessions?)

2. Pray that your church would not fall into the trap of trying to dedicate resources and services to God that cost you nothing.

Guideline #11: Begin with a Prayer for Sanctification

Applicability

- **Target Populations:** This has multilevel applicability
    1. Your church body as an entity
    2. Any ministry spawned by your church body, and
    3. The rank and file church member

Exodus 31:13: .... *that you may know that I am the LORD who sanctifies you.*

Leviticus 20:8: ... *I am the LORD who sanctifies you.*

Leviticus 21:8b: ... *for I the LORD, who sanctify you, am holy.*

Leviticus 21:15: ... *for I the Lord sanctify him.*

Leviticus 21:23: ... *for I the LORD sanctify them.*

Leviticus 22:9: ... *I the LORD sanctify them.*

Leviticus 22:16: ... *for I the LORD sanctify them.*

Leviticus 22:32: *You shall not profane My holy name, but I will be hallowed among the children of Israel. I am the LORD who sanctifies you,*

Topical Delineation and Elaboration

Reciprocity?

How is this guideline different from a prayer of dedication? What does sanctification do for our Christian service? Why should we seek to attain it?

When Jacob dedicated himself to God, God reciprocated by sanctifying Jacob – despite his glaring flaws. Remember, before there was God's law, sin was in the world. In other words, God overlooked a lot of sins committed by the inhabitants of that day. If the truth is known, there is probably a lot more of that kind of grace going on in our day and time than we realize.

Membership Focus: *A vital principle you can apply to your church from Jacob's story is that God will not be limited or constrained by our flaws. That should give us some encouragement when we worry about whether our shortcomings limit our ministries' success. As long as we maintain our devotion to those ministries, God is able. That, however, doesn't mean we should be cavalier or have a flippant attitude about our flaws.*

Or Quid Pro Quo?

Discussions about sanctification usually turn to consecration. Of the various sources I researched, different ministries define these terms differently. They can't just give a concise definition; they have to deliver a protracted dissertation to justify their point of view. In that regard, I doubt that God will withhold blessings from your new work just because you don't have an academic understanding of these two terms. So, I'm going with the definition that consecration is man's side of the equation in setting himself apart for God's work (i.e., the act of dedication). And sanctification is God's side of the equation by culminating the deed of being set apart (i.e., making your new ministry holy and acceptable to Him). If the thought of making you and your ministry holy doesn't scare some sobriety into you, then_____. (you fill in the blank).

Membership Focus Part A: *The benefit of being set apart is that you will recognize and appreciate your God-given uniqueness. We have already touched on this point under Noah. It also means that you will have the <u>capacity</u> to minister like no other church. That's because you are committed to being and doing all the things Jesus has called you to do. This capacity, like faith, is an attribute God instills in us. It's not something we self-generate by simply dedicating ourselves. Because God has set your church body apart, no one can do it quite the way you do. That should be true irrespective of your church's size or denomination.*

Membership Focus Part B: *The degree to which you achieve <u>your apartness</u> also reflects your obedience to God's word. We can then assert that sanctification is pointless without consecration. By interpretation, your apartness is meaningless if you are not obedient to submit to that end. When you are consecrated and sanctified, you will also develop a sensitivity toward sin. Your church will be known as a repentant church. You will quickly forgive and have a reputation for being forgiving as well. Jesus reminded His followers that the real litmus test is that the world <u>will know you are My disciples if you have love for one another.</u> (Jn. 13:35)*

Eventually, the Buses Stop Running

Churches that practice under the covering of sanctification are careful to give God all the glory for their blessings and successes. They tend to glorify the Father from their earliest beginnings. They continue to praise Him as opposed to honoring man throughout their ministry.

Membership Focus: *If you are reading this in hindsight, and the door has not been closed on your opportunity, the time to consecrate (dedicate) yourself is now, before you go one step further. God is the premier mover and shaker. He can redirect and reconstruct without missing a beat. Suppose your door is open, but you haven't started moving toward it. Your first act is to position yourself through consecration before moving through the door. If your door is closed, and you know it because someone else will possess the ministry, then take it as a lesson learned and pray for your next open door.*

Key Insights for Prayer:

1. Pray that your church would have a *"faith sense"* of the *capacity* God has endowed you with and not fear the exercise of that capacity.

2. As your church progressively emulates a sanctified church, pray that the congregation at large would understand the higher standard to which God has called them. That entails a concerted effort to espouse such ideals without dishonoring the Name of God by violating the same. That's a fancy way of saying, "don't talk the talk if you are not going to walk the walk." That's what I mean by not being cavalier or flippant about your flaws.

Life Event Number 4 - Jacob

That brings us to the end of Jacob, so let us collect our prayer pointers before moving on to Joseph.

Summary List of Prayer Pointers from Jacob

- Pray that God will fully release you from lingering relics of your past. Pray for the dissolution of barriers and perceptions that keep you in the prison of your past.

- Pray that God will enable your leadership to see beyond obstacles the enemy throws in the road to block you from fulfilling God's calling.

- Pray that God would give you and your fellow congregants the freedom to wrestle with Him on issues with which you wrestle.

- Pray that God will give you and your church the capacity to be fully devoted and willing to commit all of your material possessions if called upon to do so.

- Pray that your church would not fall into the trap of trying to dedicate resources and services to God that cost you nothing.

- Pray that your church would have a "faith sense" of the capacity God has endowed you with and not fear the exercise of that capacity.

- As your church progressively emulates a sanctified church, pray that the congregation at large would understand the higher standard to which God has called them. That entails a concerted effort to espouse such ideals without dishonoring the Name of God by violating the same. Don't talk the talk if you are not going to walk the walk. That's what I mean by not being cavalier or flippant about your flaws.

Life Event Number 4 - Jacob

Life Event Number 5 – JOSEPH

The Genesis saga of beginnings closes with our final patriarch of the faith. His name is Joseph. Joseph was a man of vision and integrity. That is how he was able to become such a noble ruler and administrator. As a side note, Joseph's story takes up 26% of the book of Genesis? Joseph stands out as a sterling example of how every spiritual leader should set their course. The following five guidelines go hand in hand and are, therefore, in rapid-fire succession. You can't take the good ones and leave the unpleasant ones behind; they are a packaged deal. As such, all five guidelines will apply to the same target groups.

Guideline #12: Begin with Vision

Applicability

- **Target Populations:**
    1. Your leadership
    2. Your church body as an entity

Proverbs 29:18: *Where there is no revelation, the people cast off restraint;*

Ezekiel 40:2: In the visions of God He took me into the land of Israel and set me on a very high mountain; on it toward the south was something like the structure of a city.

Acts 2:17: And it shall come to pass in the last days, says God, That I will pour out of My Spirit on all flesh; ..., Your young men shall see visions, Your old men shall dream dreams.

Topical Delineation and Elaboration

Cool for Joseph

Joseph is generally known for the two very literal visions he saw as a lad. Both were in symbolic imagery, with the central theme that Joseph becomes ruler over his entire family. In one dream, he saw the sun, moon, and eleven stars bow down to him. Joseph didn't have to interpret the dream to his family; they were quite clear on its meaning. The sun and the moon were his parents, and the 11 stars were all of his brothers. In another vision where he and his brothers were reaping grain, his brother's sheaves bowed down to his sheaf. After Joseph was promoted to a position second to Pharaoh over all of Egypt, the symbolism in his dreams materialized as he visualized them. His brothers visited him at a time of real need in their lives. And with time, his entire family bowed down and paid homage to him, Just as foretold in his dreams. That must have been quite a moment for him.

Membership Focus: *God may not bless you with such glory-filled visions, but He still gives them in various forms. Don't, however, wait for one as dramatic as Joseph's as a signal to move out. The vision for your church will probably come to your pastor, and it may be a mental conceptualization as simple as the analogy between vitamins and fitness. I quote Ezekiel for this guideline to* *convey that God may cast a tangible vision to represent an abstract aspect of the ministry He has for your church. For example, the visual image He gave my pastor to start the new church campus in Cypress, Texas, was a flock of doves abruptly rising out of the field. It was as if to say, "this is where I want the new campus to go." And no, the doves did not form the image of a cross or the visage of Jesus.*

He could sovereignly choose to take you down this pathway as a prayer warrior who sees visions and dreams. But you do not need to see visions and dream dreams to develop the skill of praying in imagery. I love to use images such as "shattering the chains of bondage," "tearing down the high towers that imprison," or "tearing up the foundations of vain philosophies." Others include "laying waste the siege-works of the enemy," "confounding their communications," "letting them hear the sounds of battle from afar." Whatever He desires of you, pray for commitment if for no other reason than the flesh is weak. Forever be committed to His purpose and vision for your church. Without it, you shall surely perish! (Hosea 4:6)

<u>Key Insight for Prayer:</u> Pray that God will tie his vision to your purpose and forever instill it in the heart of your church as a guiding light that you will never forsake.

Bridging the Gap

In our discussion, we have come to a point where I need to bridge the gap between the personal and corporate levels. In Joseph's situation, his visions were messages from God on what *would* happen, not what *might* happen if Joseph pursued the visions. In our day and time, we tend to equate visions with callings. That is, we don't say we've received a vision from God; we say God has called us to do such and such. In this context, visions can apply equally at the corporate level and the individual level. Yet, they don't work at the corporate level if no one receives them at the personal level.

God didn't place the *First Church of Adam and Eve* in the garden. He didn't task the *Church of Noah* to build the Ark. He didn't call on the *Cathedral of Abraham* to leave its hometown and go to a foreign country where its membership would grow like the sand of the sea. He called individuals. Joseph was only one person amid the enormous family of God. While he didn't call corporate entities in the Old Testament, He calls corporate entities under the New Testament covenant, in a limited sense. You can render it in terms of a calling on your church for a specific task. In reality, God is calling your pastor and expecting his flock to fall in line.

Now here is the critical concept I want you to wrap your head around. The Old Testament individuals God called were typically in some spiritual leadership role, somewhat akin to a priest (yes, Jacob also). By contrast, under the New Testament covenant, we are a kingdom of priests. You could say that He has called all of us *individually*, but primarily in context with our *corporate bond* (1st Peter 2:5). So, each church functions as an entity because of the combined contributions of the members. It's the only form of circular logic that works. You are only one individual, and so am I, and that is what God works through, individuals. Our church matters to God because we all matter to God.

Key Insight for Prayer: Pray that God will convict every committed Christian in your church to take ownership of the vision given to your pastor. Pray that commitment is seared into their hearts to see that vision through to fruition.

Guideline #13: Begin in the Face of Adversity

Applicability

Job 2:10b: *Shall we indeed accept good from God, and shall we not accept adversity?*

Ecclesiastes 7:14: *In the day of prosperity be joyful, but in the day of adversity consider: Surely God has appointed the one as well as the other, so that man can find out nothing that will come after him.*

Topical Delineation and Elaboration

Why the Road is Less Traveled

Beginning a new work, a new ministry, or a new church for God will not make you immune to problems. Sometimes we think doing the Lord's work will shield us from troubles and woes. Isn't the Great I Am looking after us? If we are doing the Lord's work, won't this insulate us from hardship? While the answer to those questions is yes, our protection doesn't play out the way we think it should. Anyone involved in Christian service for very long will say that you are guaranteed to experience just the opposite. Yes, you may be a trailblazer. Yes, you will likely take a road not taken. Unfortunately, yes, your greatest fear that the road will be fraught with difficulties and obstacles will probably also come true.

Not exactly what you wanted to hear, and granted, I'm acting a bit impish, but there are two points here. First, don't go gleefully into a ministry unaware that you may get ambushed. Maybe you will, perhaps you won't, but it's wise to prepare. Being mentally and emotionally prepared to be blindsided is part of counting the costs. Second, no one should base their decision to pursue a ministry primarily on the inevitability of obstacles that might arise along the way. That can be a factor but shouldn't be the deciding factor. Pause for a moment and clear that negative perspective out of your mind. Now here is the positive encouragement I will use to reinforce the following counsel. Let the *end* goal be the weightier factor, not the *journey*. For all you know, you might have a glide path to your finish line. The means to an end can be fickle and unpredictable, so don't try to second-guess what the road will be like when making your decision to pursue a ministry initiative.

My pastor's decision to launch the Cypress Church illustrates my point. He encountered tremendous resistance, but the end goal outweighed the suffering he endured on the way to that goal. My husband and I once launched a Children's Church before they were fashionable. Like the Cypress Church, we ran into resistance from those who thought a child's primary role was to behave in Big Church (a child's rendition of the adult church). But the end goal was worth it. At the other extreme, my husband launched a recreational ministry for an apartment complex near our church. That just sailed on through with no problems.

On the lighter side, let me give you a real-life illustration you will find humorous. Hurricane Rita was bearing down on the Texas Gulf Coast in 2005. Houston residents were in mortal fear that it would wreak havoc on Houston just like Hurricane Katrina did on New Orleans a month earlier. In an unprecedented act never before witnessed in Texas, most of Houston's and Galveston's populations evacuated north toward Dallas and west toward San Antonio or Austin. It was an act never before seen because most Texans are somewhat bull-headed and refuse to evacuate under hurricane conditions. My husband and I packed our son, our three beagles, and my mother-in-law into our 1990 Toyota Camry station wagon and headed north. Our destination was a cousin who lived north of Dallas – approximately 250 miles away. About 20 hours later, my mother-in-law asked where we were. I replied, "We are still in the Woodlands" (about 30 miles outside Houston). That's how backed-up traffic was on Interstate 45. We eventually made it to our cousin's house, but that was the worst trip I have ever endured. Hurricane Rita didn't even come close to Houston. I would gladly weather a hurricane than go on another trip like that. What's the lesson here? Our objective was to get my mother-in-law out of harm's way because she was elderly. We chose *not to stay* in Houston in <u>anticipation of </u>hardships brought on by the hurricane but *decided to* evacuate in favor of what we thought would be an uneventful trip to Dallas. We unnecessarily endured abject misery out of fear of what might happen, not what did happen. As it turns out, we would have been entirely safe in Houston. So, let your end goal prioritize the hardships you are willing to endure in achieving that goal.

Key Insights for Prayer:

Pray that all ministry participants from the top down

1. will embrace the inevitability of unexpected obstacles and derailments in pursuing any ministry initiative
2. will consider the benefits of the ministry's end goal to outweigh the setbacks and delays that are sure to come.

Seriously, it is a legitimate question to ask why God allows His saints to suffer tribulation because we are supposed to be new creatures in Christ. We can make convincing arguments as to why unregenerate humanity should suffer because they are reaping what they sew, but why Christians. Besides James' *"Count it all joy"* encouragement, let me give you food for thought. Start with the question of when you think God should step in and mitigate Christian suffering. I'm not asking when God should step in; I'm asking when *you think* He should step in and stop the agony. Now follow that line of thinking to its logical conclusion. I'll pause for a minute while you do that mental exercise. You should have arrived at the logical endpoint: why doesn't God usher in the Kingdom of heaven right now? That, of course, begs the question of why He didn't bring in the kingdom 50 or 100 years ago. Well, since He hasn't, where does that leave us? None of us can fathom why God lets us suffer more than we deem reasonable. Since we don't have much say in the matter, we should accept James' admonition and keep moving forward.

Think of adversity and problems we face in daily living. Contrast that with hardship experienced by various Bible characters. You can probably think of a good number who met them head-on in God's grace. Daniel, Moses, and Job might come to mind. And definitely, Joseph fits this profile. His family, personal liberty, and human worth, and dignity were all taken from him. Yet, he continued to serve God from the beginning of his life right up until the end of it. What was his secret? Shouldn't it be clear?

He Respected God Above All Else!!!

Are these patriarchs of the faith not set before us as examples in withstanding hardship?

There Are No Storms in Spiritual Clouds

If the grace of God is what got Joseph past his brothers' betrayal and past his jail time, then we, too, will need that same grace. When I speak of grace here, I'm not using it in its narrow sense of receiving something we don't deserve. That doesn't fit the narrative of needing God's grace to navigate through trials. I speak in the broadest meaning of the kindness of God toward man. As servants of the Most-High God, we too can rest upon the Lord's unchangeable abiding grace in moving us toward our goal. Let's Come down out of the spiritual clouds we have been abiding in and consider the reality of Christian living. I'm referring to day-to-day struggles and hardships at home, work, and play. These struggles threaten to derail us in our quest to achieve God's vision and purpose for our personal lives and church. What can we do as prayer warriors when we encounter adversity? Let me demonstrate by continuing with the story of my pastor's vision.

My Pastor presented his vision to the church, fully expecting them to buy into it with utter enthusiasm and fall into lockstep with him to purchase the property. And *that's* when things went south. Blowback began to surface to prevent him from seeing his dream come true. That was when a coordinated effort arose from opponents of the new vision. But these weren't contrarian church members; they were well-meaning folk who thought they stood in the right and believed the pastor to be misguided. But so thought the pastor and his proponents about the opponents of his vision.

Let me pause here with a claimer - that's the opposite of a disclaimer. Under the right circumstances, I could have been drawn into one camp as I was into the other. I will tie up this testimonial at the end of this discussion.

Let's continue with our story. There was a third party involved in this war - an invisible third party. The adversary had a plan all his own too. Satan did not want to see all those hundreds of lost individuals come to know the Lord, so he used man to interfere with God's plan. As we progress through this narrative, I would ask you to let another verse drum through your head - *For we do not wrestle against flesh and blood, but against principalities, against powers, against the rulers of the darkness of this age, against spiritual hosts of wickedness in the heavenly places. (Eph 6:12)*. Satan cleverly put his plan to work in the hearts of some of the trusted leaders in our church. He whacked them hard with a healthy dose of logistical constraints in the form of Luke 14:28. He convinced them that we did not have the money to begin building another campus. Because they were very talented and intelligent businessmen, they naturally leaned toward a business perspective and a practical mindset.

Our pastor, however, did not visualize the project with a businessman's mentality. In Adam and Eve, we discussed how God instills in us the talents necessary to do His plan. But the enemy can hijack those same talents to work against God's plans. Keep in mind that I'm talking about skills we come into this world with, not spiritual gifts we receive when we get saved. Well, Satan hasn't remained ignorant during the thousands of years he's been on this earth. He knew how to turn those same talents to work against God's plans. It's straightforward; Satan blindsided them with Biblical half-truths like, "remember when Jesus said, "consider the costs." You need to take this one by sight, leave the faith for times when the way is clear, and the outcome is certain." When we don't take Ephesians 6:12 seriously or when we believe it applies to the other fellow, that is the day we open ourselves to be ambushed by the enemy. That's when the enemy can walk right in, practically in plain sight, and recruit all the well-meaning but unsuspecting believers into doing his bidding.

Their temporary blindness caused them to raise undue alarm and concern among the members of the church. They also went to visit the pastor and tried to persuade him to discontinue the building program. Our pastor countered by explaining that numerous other folks in the congregation were of a much different opinion. They had already bound with one another in agreement with God, asking Him to enlarge their faith to get the job done in God's perfect timing. The detractors argued that it was not yet the Master's time. Ooh, I didn't think it was allowed to invoke the Lord's name when arguing both sides of an issue. They were very adamant about their viewpoint and beliefs. Their conviction was firm, causing them to create a faction within the church body. They made one last appeal to the pastor with the threat of leaving the church and withdrawing their financial support. Our pastor said CIAO. He could not go along with their idea of halting the pursuit of the new vision.

Unfortunately, they proceeded with their threat and left every facet of their ministry behind. Some members took their entourage and started churches of their own. I knew only a few of those who left, and I didn't know them that well, so I intentionally elected not to follow up on where they landed or how they prospered. For me, that would have been an open door for the flesh. And to the credit of those that stayed, I never heard one person even whisper a word of what happened, much less gossip about it. It was as though a split had never taken place.

My Dilemma

Now let me close the loop on my earlier claimer. If I had landed in a different network of friends and acquaintances, I would have sympathized with the naysayers. I cannot credit my exceptional spiritual maturity or superior spiritual enlightenment (I'm being facetious again). It appears to have been fate that I landed in a social circle aligned with the pastor. You see, our relationships have a potent influence on how we view issues in life – for right or wrong. We tend to formulate our opinions and philosophical positions by those with whom we associate. Suppose someone says the social circle I landed in wasn't fate but was of God. That may be so, but what does that say of well-meaning people who landed in the opposing social circles? Was that of God too? That's a Catch-22 question I would prefer to leave alone.

As noted above, I can say from personal experience that the naysayers I knew weren't rabble-rousers or contentious disruptors before it all started. They appeared to be good Bible teachers and good people – maybe overly pragmatic, but good people (as man gauges good). My point is that I don't want to come across as so smug as to presume I'm exceptional in having landed in the right camp. I don't want to be so careless as to say I'm immune to being blindsided by Satan. Hence, the caution appropriate for me is, *beware lest you also fall from your own steadfastness being led away with the error of the wicked.* (2nd Peter 3: 17)

Philosophical question: This goes back to the last paragraph in Guideline #2 under Noah. Who do you believe when both factions invoke God's name in their justification of their position? The Pastor and his followers think the Lord is leading them to step out now. The detractors and their followers say it's not the Lord's timing. One could argue that we should believe the Pastor because he is God's spokesman. But just because he is the pastor does that mean he can't be wrong? I tend to err on the side of supporting the pastor, even at the risk of being in error. He is the one who is supposed to be God's spokesman. That's where the Prayer Warriors come in.

Key Insights for Prayer:

1. Ask God to provide multiple threads of circumstantial evidence to make His will clear to the Pastor so that he would not succumb to reasoned arguments from the opposition.

2. Ask God to place a noticeable anointing on your pastor that shows He is with your pastor when opposition or adversity arises.

3. Ask God to give people the objectivity to prevent personal loyalties from clouding their recognition of God's vision for the church.

We should give no quarter to confusion in the body of Christ. The fallout of antiauthoritarianism can prove to be a disaster. That is because antiauthoritarianism embodies the spirit of divisiveness. It describes efforts to go against God's anointed, namely our pastor. The scriptures clearly and strictly forbid this kind of activity.

Storm? What Storm?

Getting back to our story, the contrast of walking by faith and not by sight had a much different result for our pastor and his loyal members. God gave them untold prosperity to open up an additional church campus for God's glory. That campus has continued to grow and prosper in winning the lost and receiving new members into their family fellowship.

So why am I sharing this faith walk with you? It serves as an example to all intercessors everywhere. It emphasizes how the spirit-filled church can never be spirit-filled and achieved its goal without prayer. Prayer and intercession behind the scenes were the secrets to our success. Generous and sacrificial giving also played a part in witnessing the fulfillment of God's vision for our church. But would sacrificial giving have been possible without the prayers?

Membership Focus: *What might this mean for you? To some people, obstacles are like a "Do Not Enter" sign or an "Employees Only" sign. It's a clear message to stop and come no further. To others, obstacles are a triple-dog-dare to challenge the opposition. How do you distinguish between the two? Let me answer with a question. Have you settled in your heart whether God appointed the work your church is undertaking? Then there is your answer. If we can't know the answer to that question, then how can we claim to adhere to Hebrews 11:6:*

But without faith it is impossible to please Him, for he who comes to God <u>must believe that He is</u>, and that He is a rewarder of those who diligently seek Him.

<u>Key Insight for Prayer:</u> Pray that opposition or adversity would not generate doubt as to whether your pastor indeed heard the Lord correctly in the first place.

Guideline #14: Begin with Tenacity & Perseverance

<u>Applicability</u>

Romans: 5:3-4: *And not only that, but we also glory in tribulations, knowing that tribulation produces perseverance; and perseverance, character; and character, hope.*

Topical Delineation and Elaboration

Seeing Beyond His Troubles

Despite what his brothers had put him through, Joseph knew it was far more critical that he stay on task and pay homage to the Lord and not to mere Man. Joseph remained committed to God's purpose and attendant visions throughout his entire life. In reading the Genesis passage, we can discover another significant truth. He stayed true to his God-given vision even when the future seemed hopeless. Joseph went through some pretty dark and dismal trials, yet he remained faithful and true to God. What a message to us all! That is, to all us saints who make up the church.

Are Obstacles Just Distractions?

Let's take a break here and do another mental exercise. Think of events in your life, small or great, in which you gave up because obstacles got in the way. That is to say, the price demanded by the challenges was not worth the objective you were trying to achieve. Of all the ones you can call to mind, were there any for which you questioned whether or not you should have given up? In retrospect, did you realize any were God-given opportunities you let slip away? But you acquiesced, believing it should have been easier if God meant it to be?

On the other hand, how many can you recall when you were justified in not paying the price because it wasn't worth it after all? So much uncertainty can surround opportunities. Are obstacles God's way of testing our resolve, or are they God's way of telling us the door is closed? We could probably hear testimony after testimony that would justify both viewpoints and would cover every conceivable combination of scenarios involving obstacles and opposition from within and opposition from outside. But it all boils down to one thing. How certain are you that God provided the vision? Does your spirit bear witness with His Spirit that the opportunity is genuine? I echo my earlier statement; the answer is that circumstances and obstacles should not establish your decision. Whether or not your spirit bears witness with God's Spirit should determine your decision.

<u>Key Insights for Prayer:</u>

1. Pray that God will give you and your church discernment on how to address obstacles and opposition.
2. Pray for certainty in all of your visions and open doors so that your church would forge ahead with tenacity, especially in the face of opposition or adversity.

Guideline #15: Begin with Integrity

<u>Applicability</u>

Job 2:3: *Have you considered My servant Job, that there is none like him on the earth, a blameless and upright man, one who fears God and shuns evil? And still he holds fast to his integrity, although you incited Me against him, to destroy him without cause.*

Job 27:5: *Far be it from me that I should say you are right; Till I die I will not put away my integrity from me.*

Life Event Number 5 - Joseph

Topical Delineation and Elaboration

Let's Take Stock

Joseph emulated still another aspect of godliness. He knew how crucial it was that he strives toward righteous living. For our narrative, we will call that integrity. He also knew that his moral purity was part of this process. He did not succumb to sin when Potiphar's wife attempted to seduce him. He did not get into petty reprisals when Pharaoh's cupbearer remembered his fault. And lastly, he did not dish out a healthy dose of payback when his brothers arrived at his loading dock. That certainly must have been a surreal experience. I believe, however, he enjoyed rattling his brothers' cage with the antics he pulled before revealing himself.

When we look at his life in review, we can unequivocally affirm the following. Having been put through the wringer, he was abased to the point that he could give none other than God credit for his elevated position. Let's quickly reprise Joseph's life with a tongue in cheek commentary:

- His brothers attempted to kill him by throwing him into a pit (he must have tattled on them a lot – a child's version of integrity).

- They changed their mind and sold him into slavery (win-win, they get cash, Joseph regains his life, he just doesn't get to go home).

- Potiphar's wife (what was her name anyway) sets him up for a no-win situation. (Potiphar would have caught them eventually; Joseph made the right no-win choice).

- He spends time in jail (I've heard those were nasty dungeon-like places).

- The chief butler and chief baker get thrown into prison and have their dreams interpreted by Joseph. They do not return the favor when they get out (serves the baker right).

- He spends more time in jail (bright spot, he gains special treatment from the jailer by this time)

- Butler finally remembers Joseph when Pharaoh has a dream (may give a clue as to why the Butler wound up in jail in the first place)

- Joseph achieves celebrity status (that just had to have been like one of those sling-shot rides at the amusement parks).

Let me tie together this guideline and Guideline #12. Vision sets the goal, but honor and integrity set the rules of engagement for achieving that goal. Without integrity, vision and purpose take the path of the flesh. If Joseph had not clung to his honor, would he have ever been able to achieve God's vision for his life? Or would his life have looked a lot different? It is his honor that got him a trusted position in Potiphar's house. It was his integrity that won him an elevated status in prison. And it was his honor that earned him a *trusted* title with Pharaoh himself. (Proverbs 11:3: *The integrity of the upright will guide them, but the perversity of the unfaithful will destroy them.*)

Cause or Effect?

So! Was the integrity he exhibited inherent to his character or was it developed through his circumstances. I believe it was intrinsic in an infantile state; he just didn't express it very well as a youth. For

Life Event Number 5 - Joseph

him to tattle on his brothers showed that he had high expectations of how people should behave, and in the case of his brothers, he acted when they didn't. So, the question of whether he started this way would merit a "qualified" yes. But the question of whether his integrity was a result of his circumstances would warrant a <u>definite</u> yes. The attribute of integrity and how it matures is a curious process. We can definitively say that he was shaped into his heightened sense of integrity by what he suffered. But by the same token, I firmly believe that his inherent sense of integrity was one of the attributes that got him through his suffering. But was it the only factor involved? Did his innate sense of integrity give rise to his *willingness* to endure affliction?

Let's shift gears. If Joseph had not had those dreams as a youth, would he have ever had the tenacity to endure the trials he sustained? He could easily have said, "why am I standing up for what is right when no one else is?" The answer is no; integrity is not what gave rise to his willingness to endure the suffering. Faith was - the substance of something dreamed (hoped for), the knowledge (evidence) of something yet to come (unseen). The *conviction* that somehow, someday, God would bring it to pass is what drove Joseph. Still, the integrity God instilled in him took him on the path of being esteemed by Potiphar, preferred by the jailer, and ultimately favored by Pharaoh. After all, Joseph could have extorted Pharaoh by telling him just enough to whet his curiosity, but he didn't.

Food for thought. Joseph told Pharaoh that his duplicity of dreams meant God established it. Do you suppose that interpretation dawned on Joseph at the moment he was listening to Pharaoh's dreams? Joseph had duplicate visions, but there was no mention of what that meant when those dreams occurred. Now granted, Joseph hadn't achieved his elevated status when he was interpreting Pharaoh's dreams. But the mere fact that he went from prison to Pharaoh in practically a heartbeat may have given him the realization that it was all starting to happen.

Membership Focus: *Maybe that bit of speculation is of little importance, but maybe it's not. What is important is that God does reinforce His callings by iterative events or experiences. Look for these in everyday life.*

Noah De Ja Vu

So, can we discern a governing hierarchy here? I propose that Joseph's dreams gave rise to his faith which served as the *"why"* (dominant factor) he endured the trials. We will call this *vision-based faith*. The dreams created a vested interest in his reaching the destination God had set for him. The vested interest gave rise to integrity. That, in turn, served as the *"intermediary"* (subdominant factor) for forging ahead in the face of overwhelming adversity. We will call this *vision-based integrity*. It's starting to sound like Noah deja vu.

Integrity propelled him through suffering, producing an outcome of greater integrity. Without the visions, I'm not sure he would have ever stuck with it to the degree that he did. We can say the dreams he received are equivalent to the visceral component of Noah's sense of purpose. It is Joseph's equivalent of having skin in the game. In every adverse situation he found himself in, he could have responded in a manner that would have made his life a lot more miserable. Thus, making his faith a lot less attractive. That is not to say he had the power to sabotaged God's plans; he didn't. But if he had tried, God would have had to pull a whole lot more rabbits out of the hat than he did with Abraham, Isaac, and Jacob combined.

As with the idea of visions or callings, integrity applies at two levels: the personal and corporate levels. And as with visions and callings, integrity doesn't work at the corporate level if we don't practice it at the individual level. Our collective moral character and our combined integrity contribute to our integrity on a corporate level. Our churches can only have the same high standards on a corporate level if we practice these values at the individual level. Case in point, when your church publicizes a policy that welcomes all, do you as an individual try and meet that standard? Or do you exempt yourself with the expectation that someone will receive them? As such, our personal testimony matters a great deal to God. Why? Because we are Christ's representatives here on earth.

There is no place where this representation shines so clearly as in the church. We will never be sinless until glory, but we should stand out in the crowd. Our moral character and our integrity should always reflect the nature of God as much as possible. Our mission should reflect Christ in all that we say, think, or do as a part of our daily living. Adopting high standards, values, and moral character will require us to walk in integrity. Let's not be a fulfillment of Romans 2:24: *For the name of God is blasphemed among the Gentiles because of you.* Our efforts and behavior should begin and end with honesty and truthfulness.

Membership Focus: *You can probably think of many different areas to which this applies in association with your church membership. One of them might be in your business dealings with the outside world. For example, your church may be purchasing additional land as they grow in number and size. A congregation should give the property owner a fair and reasonable asking price.*

Everyone expects price negotiations in the process of arriving at a fair price, but taking advantage of a seller's desperation is not appropriate. Who knows, there may be someone else out there vying for the same property and who will negotiate a price more agreeable to the seller. You don't want to miss God's opportunity because you were trying to nickel and dime the seller to death.

Here is another point regarding integrity. If you are purchasing property for a new church in the suburbs, avoid all appearance of competition with other churches doing the same. To the World, it smacks of petty differences and insincerity. I know the first thought that may jump into your head is, "they are invading our territory and taking our ministry away from us." I rest my case. You don't want your ministry's target community thinking they are nothing more than a possession or a trophy.

<u>Key Insight for Prayer:</u> Pray that every church member understands that they are on display for the world to see and that they need to take their integrity seriously.

Guideline #16: Begin with a Pinch of Humility

<u>Applicability</u>

Proverbs 15:33 – *The fear of the LORD is the instruction of wisdom, and before honor is humility*

1st Peter 5:5b - *Yes, all of you be submissive to one another, and be clothed with humility, for "God resists the proud but gives grace to the humble."*

Life Event Number 5 - Joseph

Topical Delineation and Elaboration

Life's Not Fair, but is it Just?

When Joseph was a boy, I believe he was just an arrogant, spoiled brat. It was no secret that his father Jacob favored him and showed it by giving him a coat of many colors. By contrast, as second in command of all Egypt, Joseph was able to do actual harm to his brothers when they visited him. Instead, he met the real need in their lives and the life of Jacob. Reiterating, he knew it was far more imperative that he and his family pay homage to the Lord and not to mere Man. Joseph demonstrated this by fully forgiving his brothers, who had been so cruel and spiteful to him. Never once did he take revenge upon them. Joseph stayed committed to God's purpose and vision for his entire life.

What happened? The answer is simple. Joseph was knocked down and kicked, not once, not twice but three times. That is what it took to knock the arrogance out of him. That experience taught him the world is not fair, and the world at large somehow missed the favored status he had at home. He was exceptional to no one outside of Jacob's household. And within the family of Jacob, he was special only to Jacob. The net result of that experience was humility. Just plain ol' unembellished humility. No faux modesty, no crocodile tears, no beating of the breast and saying, "I'm thankful I'm not like this sinner over here," just unadulterated humility. That is the only explanation of how he was abruptly catapulted to second in command in Egypt and not be bitter or vengeful toward his brothers, Potiphar, or Pharaoh's cupbearer.

We have difficulty comprehending Joseph's response throughout his ordeal because humility is a foreign concept to many of us; it just does not compute. That was one of God's intended endpoints for Joseph. When God accomplished the desired degree of humility in Joseph, He gave him beauty for ashes.

Membership Focus: *Only our heavenly father can give us beauty for ashes. God is the one person who can take something utterly adverse and yet turn it into something good for His glory. Suffering adversity doesn't have to mean God is trying to knock the pride out of us. I don't even think we need to know the reason why we are going through adversity. God knows, and that is all that is important. He knows when to turn the oven off. We only need to simply trust him to know how to order and arrange our circumstances. Praise His name and His creative ability. He is a terrific God and a tremendous creator.*

Key Insight for Prayer: Pray that God will do whatever is necessary to instill humility in our church leaders' lives. As we said before, as the leadership goes, so goes the congregation.

The Ball's in Your Court Now

Prayer is the vehicle that will help us get in touch with the spiritual reality, which transcends our physical reality. Reviewing the story of Joseph can significantly facilitate this process. We have presented four ingredients in his life that we can replicate as members of the body of Christ: vision, tenacity, integrity, and humility. All four have a role to play in weathering affliction. Vision and humility serve as bookends to adversity. Integrity and tenacity, in their initial infantile state, are shaped and strengthened through suffering. Integrating these qualities into our prayers will, in turn, assist the entire church body as a whole. God elevated this one-time youth from slavery to worldwide leadership and rulership. What a remarkable transition! He can do the same for us, but we must adhere to Churchill's adage. "Never give in, never give in, never, never, never, never—in nothing, great or small, large or petty—never give in except to convictions of honor and good sense."(1941).

Throughout this discussion, you may have wondered why I didn't include dream interpretation as a significant element in Joseph's cache of skills. That is because dreams and the ability to interpret them were how God equipped Joseph; these weren't skills he developed. God prepared and raised up Joseph for this purpose. We should address dreams and their interpretation the same way visions are addressed: as something given at God's discretion, not necessarily at our request or on-demand. God does, however, equip us with special skills to carry out our calling or ministry vision. The lesson we learn from Joseph is how he developed as a person over a lifetime by being true to his ability to dream and interpret dreams.

Membership Focus: *The lesson we should personalize is to develop spiritually by being true to how God has equipped us. Maybe you aren't gifted to interpret dreams. Whatever gift God has invested in you, however, that is your vision. From that vision, you can develop faith, you can build integrity, you can grow in tenacity, and you can cultivate humility. Most importantly, He has equipped you with the skills and motivation necessary to push into the unknown. He has outfitted you to endure opposition and exercise strengths your church may need to see their new work culminate in fruition.*

Key Insight for Prayer: Pray that visions and callings are taken seriously at the individual and corporate levels. Pray that the evidence is clear. They are a sign God has endowed us with the capabilities to pursue our calling.

In closing out the book of Genesis, we can see it is a marvelous and insightful book. It's been gratifying to delineate some of the incredible truths presented in it. It has taken me back to many instances in my own life when I felt I hardly knew where to begin in the plans God was making for my family and me. Hopefully, I've opened new vistas to you in recognizing whether your church is on track or not. I feel like I've given it to you as I received it from the Lord.

Summary List of Prayer Pointers from Joseph

- Pray that God will tie his vision to your purpose and forever instill it in the heart of your church as a guiding light that you will never forsake.

- Pray that God will convict every committed Christian in your church to take ownership of the vision given to your pastor. Pray that commitment is seared into their hearts to see that vision through to fruition.

- Pray that all ministry participants from the top down will embrace the inevitability of unexpected obstacles and derailments in pursuing any ministry initiative.

- Pray that all ministry participants from the top down will consider the benefits of the ministry's end goal to outweigh the setbacks and delays that are sure to come.

- Ask God to provide multiple threads of circumstantial evidence to make His will clear to the pastor so that he would not succumb to reasoned arguments from the opposition.

- Ask God to place a noticeable anointing on your pastor that shows He is with your pastor when opposition or adversity arises.

- Ask God to give people the objectivity to prevent personal loyalties from clouding their recognition of God's vision for the church.

- Pray that opposition or adversity would not generate doubt as to whether your pastor indeed heard the Lord correctly in the first place.

- Pray that God will give you and your church discernment on how to address obstacles and opposition.

- Pray for certainty in all of your visions and open doors so that your church would forge ahead with tenacity, especially in the face of opposition or adversity.
- Pray that every church member understands that they are on display for the world to see and that they need to take their integrity seriously.
- Pray that God will do whatever is necessary to instill humility in our church leaders' lives because, as the leadership goes, so goes the congregation.
- Pray that visions and callings are taken seriously at the individual and corporate levels. Pray that the evidence is clear; they are a sign God has endowed us with the capabilities to pursue our calling.

Life Event Number 5 - Joseph

Life Event Number 5 - Joseph

A Prayer from the Book of Genesis

How shall we then begin?

Ever watching and listening to what we once were and have been.

Praise God for His many blessings and answered prayers.

Go forth in boldness and take the godly dare.

Wrapped up in the garments of faith, knowing
He will always be there.

Thank Him and His guiding light and strong and gentle hand.

Though every testing and trial, we may not understand.

The Master, through each of them, will have a much deeper
and profound purpose.

His mercy and love are forever very near us.

For we will build on a secure and everlasting foundation.

No work we perform will be without
the slightest bit of hesitation.

The savior will, at all times, be our solid rock.

Even when the nonbelieving

Will sometimes His beloved cause mock.

We ask for true belief and unfailing trust

Knowing and meditating on His word will be a must.

His promises are so very dependable and sure.

We'll not look too much to man, part of Satan's schemes and evil lure.

Remembering to walk one step at a time.

Never running ahead or behind, we will walk the line.

Crucial steps we won't be missing,

May we begin at the beginning as our starting place while we seek His face.

Each of us will also be found in honesty and integrity,

Having a heart of gold that is devoid of any deception wherever we shall be.

Forsaking and not bowing to man's will,

Listening to Your voice that bids us peace, peace be still.

As Noah of old did, let us always obey.

Like him, we can't always see every detail of the big picture along the way.

May we never despise small beginnings because if we are faithful over the least of these

He will make us stewards of much more, and His abundant grace shall not cease.

A Prayer from the Book of Genesis

Impart your vision so that we see with mind's eye.

Instill in us a sense of purpose and unique identity.

For God will always have a plan.

And it will be remarkably grand.

Finally, dream big as Joseph did and let them soar up above the sky.

After all, we worship the creator of the universe, you and I.

A Prayer from the Book of Genesis

Genesis Summary

As a summary, I am reiterating the *Key Insights for Prayer* listed under each guideline.

Guideline #1: Begin with a God, not with man

➤ On a corporate level, pray that your church body

- Will make God its beginning point in all it does.
- Will not be seduced by man's philosophy of pragmatism.
- Will realize that prayer is their responsibility and domain. It is not the purview of only "the anointed," the Leadership, or the Prayer Team. It is not just the domain of those we tout as skilled in the Art of Praying.
- Will recognize when they rely on the flesh and understand the futility of relying on fleshly strength.
- Will understand the dynamic principle of living in the flesh under grace while striving to walk in the spirit.

> **At the Leadership level, pray that your church leadership**

- Can balance the role of finances in all their faith-based decisions on church operations as a whole.
- Will recognize that finances and other resources are God's vehicles to achieve His vision.
- Will spend more time seeking His guidance rather than the finances to carry out His Plan.

> **At the individual level, pray that each member**

- Will be challenged from the pulpit and from every corner of your church to live holy lives.
- Will keep short accounts with God and all they come in contact with regularly. They should be eager to prayerfully ask for cleansing and His forgiveness instead of avoiding it because they feel unworthy or unaccountable.
- Will be clothed in a spirit of humility and contrition that prompts them to repent early on when they realize they have sinned and need to make reconciliation, whether with God or Man.
- Will never forget what He saved them out of and from where they came.
- Will learn what it means to thrive under a spirit of contrition and humility versus subsisting under a perpetual burden of condemnation and guilt.
- Will see themselves as God truly sees them.

- ➤ On a grand scale,
  - Pray that every church within your sphere of influence always builds upon Christ and his Word.
  - Pray that every ministry, from its inception onward, always builds upon Christ and his Word.

Guideline #2: Begin with a Sense of Purpose

- ➤ Pray that your plans and God's plans would always be in perfect agreement.
- ➤ Pray that God will give the church leadership a spirit of discernment to recognize God's call and answer in the affirmative.
- ➤ Pray that God will give the church membership a spirit of discernment to recognize God's call and answer in the affirmative.
- ➤ Pray that your church will remain true to its vision and mission.
- ➤ Pray that your church formulates a mission statement that reflects intent as well as objective.
- ➤ Pray that your leadership will always embrace the right reason for pursuing a ministry initiative, just to obey God.

Guideline #3: Begin with The Proper Foundation

- ➤ Pray that every one of your beginnings starts with a secure foundation.
- ➤ Pray for the physical foundation upon which your church builds. Pray that the construction planners in your church

will stand firm in their conviction not to compromise when pressured to do so.

- ➢ Pray for the spiritual foundation that your church builds upon in its formative growth process. Pray that ministry participants would understand they are that foundation. The strength of that foundation is a function of scripture meditation and how they invest themselves in others.

- ➢ Pray that God will lift the fog or remove the blinders materialism and false doctrine place over the leadership's eyes.

Guideline #4: Begin with Something New

- ➢ Pray that your church can differentiate between non-negotiable principles of ministry and negotiable "how-to" methodologies in administering those principles.

- ➢ Pray that your church doesn't throw the baby out with the bathwater by forsaking timeless ministry principles on the basis that the older methodologies don't appeal to the current generation.

Guideline #5: Begin with Obedience - Do Not Despise Small Beginnings

- ➢ Pray that the saints in your church body would embrace this growth model from infancy to maturity as being ordained by God irrespective of their maturity level.

- ➢ Pray that understanding the growth process would encourage and not discourage someone's decision to submit to discipleship, start a new ministry, or even launch a new church.

- Intercede for your church's leadership and all its ministry participants to not become overly ambitious and attempt to run faster than God wants you to run. Your church leadership's near-term goals should start at the pilot program level and build from there. It's not about God's limitations but our limitations. Rest assured, your ministry will become God-size when He feels you have grown to that point.

- Pray that immature saints in your church body would not avoid discipleship out of fear that they will have to forfeit their comfort zone.

- Pray that all who have chosen to start a new ministry or submit to discipleship understand that testings and dry periods are part of the growth process. These, too, are ordained of God to produce character.

- Ask for a sense of ownership over your church's beginnings, current status, and future destiny.

- Pray for discernment of what is sacred and what is not. Holding the wrong things as sacred can derail you from advancing to greater heights.

- Pray that God would instill an attitude of sacrifice in the hearts of your church members.

- Pray for vision and innovative ideas on implementing these visions in a manner compatible with God's master plan.

- Pray that your church develops a sensitivity to God's leading to choose what stimulates growth. Pray that no failure would be in vain, but God would bring victory out of disappointment.

- ➢ Pray that the laity would forge ahead even in the face of drudgery and monotony.
- ➢ Pray that fellow saints will not falter at the task's enormity but be encouraged by the distance they have already come.

Guideline #6: Begin with Obedience – Do Not Stifle Your Faith

- ➢ Pray that we can distinguish between beneficial customs and seemingly innocuous practices that contribute nothing at best and are detrimental at worse.
- ➢ Pray that we would understand the difference between righteousness through obedience and righteousness through fulfilling the Ten Commandments, enabling us to step out in obedience, leaving the other to the Holy Spirit.
- ➢ Pray for the discernment to distinguish between legitimate faith that steps up to God's impossible and blind faith that leaps into mission impossible not ordained of God.
- ➢ Pray that God will uproot any spirit of unbelief from your church. Pray that the leadership will be willing to take on the risk of leading the charge to walk by faith.
- ➢ Pray that laity and leadership alike would step out of their fantasy world and into the reality of pursuing God's calling and purpose for your church.
- ➢ Pray that you and your church members will be prepared perfectly for the dynamics He desires to put into play for your church body.

- ➢ Pray that your church will not be detoured, derailed, or discouraged from its ordained endpoint by all the challenges that arise on the way.

Guideline #7: Begin with Proper Planning: Timing is Everything

- ➢ Ask God to instill a sense of trust in His patterns, sequence of events, and timing in the leadership.

Guideline #8: Begin in Covenant with God

- ➢ Pray that your church collectively binds together in agreement with God to accept your church's vision and purpose as ordained by Very God. Pray that they embrace that vision and purpose as being tailored specifically for your church by God Himself.

- ➢ Pray that you and your fellow congregants would be able to differentiate between sacrificing out of priorities and sacrificing out of obedience.

- ➢ Pray that you and your fellow travelers will be resolute in weathering protracted trials so that you may reap the maximum benefit in patience.

Guideline #9: Begin with A Prayer of Release from Our Past

- ➢ Pray that God will fully release you from lingering relics of your past. Pray for the dissolution of barriers and perceptions that keep you in the prison of your past.

- ➢ Pray that God will enable your leadership to see beyond obstacles the enemy throws in the road to block you from fulfilling God's calling.

➢ Pray that God would give you and your fellow congregants the freedom to wrestle with Him on issues with which you wrestle.

Guideline #10: Begin with A Prayer of Dedication

➢ Pray that God will give you and your church the capacity to be fully devoted and willing to commit all of your material possessions if called upon to do so.

➢ Pray that your church would not fall into the trap of trying to dedicate resources and services to God that cost you nothing.

Guideline #11: Begin with a Prayer for Sanctification

➢ Pray that your church would have a "faith sense" of the capacity God has endowed you with and not fear the exercise of that capacity.

➢ As your church progressively emulates a sanctified church, pray that the congregation at large would understand the higher standard to which God has called them. That entails a concerted effort to espouse such ideals without dishonoring the Name of God by violating the same. Don't talk the talk if you are not going to walk the walk. That's what I mean by not being cavalier or flippant about your flaws.

Guideline #12: Begin with a Vision

- Pray that God will tie his vision to your purpose and forever instill it in the heart of your church as a guiding light that you will never forsake.

- Pray that God will convict every committed Christian in your church to take ownership of the vision given to your pastor. Pray that commitment is seared into their hearts to see that vision through to fruition.

Guideline #13: Begin in the Face of Adversity

- Pray that all ministry participants from the top down will embrace the inevitability of unexpected obstacles and derailments in pursuing any ministry initiative.

- Pray that all ministry participants from the top down will consider the benefits of the ministry's end goal to outweigh the setbacks and delays that are sure to come.

- Ask God to provide multiple threads of circumstantial evidence to make His will clear to the pastor so that he would not succumb to reasoned arguments from the opposition.

- Ask God to place a noticeable anointing on your pastor that shows He is with your pastor when opposition or adversity arises.

- Ask God to give people the objectivity to prevent personal loyalties from clouding their recognition of God's vision for the church.

- Pray that opposition or adversity would not generate doubt as to whether your pastor indeed heard the Lord correctly in the first place.

Guideline #14: Begin with Tenacity & Perseverance

- Pray that God will give you and your church discernment on how to address obstacles and opposition.
- Pray for certainty in all of your visions and open doors so that your church would forge ahead with tenacity, especially in the face of opposition or adversity.

Guideline #15: Begin with Integrity

- Pray that every church member understands that they are on display for the world to see and that they need to take their integrity seriously.

Guideline #16: Begin with a Pinch of Humility

- Pray that God will do whatever is necessary to instill humility in our church leaders' lives because, as the leadership goes, so goes the congregation.
- Pray that visions and callings are taken seriously at the individual and corporate levels. Pray that the evidence is clear; they are a sign God has endowed us with the capabilities to pursue our calling.

www.ingramcontent.com/pod-product-compliance
Lightning Source LLC
Chambersburg PA
CBHW071955070526
44583CB00015B/1202